# COLORADO GOLD

## From the Pike's Peak Rush to the Present

Stephen M. Voynick

D0973696

Mountain Press Publishing Company
Missoula, 1992

Cover art by Bill Harrington
Cartography and illustrations by Trudi Peek

**Library of Congress Cataloging-in-Publication Data**

Voynick, Stephen M.
    Colorado gold : from the Pike's Peak rush to the present /
Stephen M. Voynick ; [cartography and illustrations by Trudi Peek].
        p.     cm.
    Includes  bibliographical references (p.      )  and index.
    ISBN 0-87842-282-X   :   $12.00
    1. Gold industry—Colorado—History.   2. Gold mines and min-
ing—Colorado—History.   3. Gold.   I. Title
HD9536.U53C68   1992                                    92-9900
338.2 ' 741 ' 09788—dc20                                 CIP

Mountain Press Publishing Company
P.O. Box 2399 • 2016 Strand Avenue
Missoula, Montana 59806
(406) 728-1900

*This book is for*
*Anne La Rocca,*
*with appreciation and thanks.*

# TABLE OF CONTENTS

*The possession of gold has ruined*
*fewer men than the lack of it.*

Thomas Bailey Aldrich
"Leaves from a Notebook" 1903

# PREFACE

If one image best symbolizes the state of Colorado, it is the familiar photograph of the gilded dome of the State Capitol Building in Denver. Behind the dome, along the western horizon, rise the Rockies, a snow-covered line of high ridges and peaks that the early explorers knew as the "shining mountains." The capitol dome reflects brilliantly with the rich luster of gold for a good reason—*it is gold*. In 1907 the entire outer surface of the 42-foot-diameter dome was covered with gold, 200 troy ounces of the yellow metal donated by Colorado mining companies and fashioned into a gleaming, film-like gold leaf. Architecturally, gold provided the crowning touch to the capitol dome; historically, the state could not have chosen a more appropriate medium.

Colorado was born with the Pike's Peak gold rush, an event triggered somewhat prematurely by modest gold discoveries made almost in the shadow of where the capitol stands today. In the fall of 1858 the nation's attention was fixed on a handful of small placer mines along the South Platte River known collectively as the "Cherry Creek diggings." Today all traces of the Cherry Creek diggings and its miners' camps are covered by the sprawl of rail yards, highways, warehouses and parking lots that surround downtown Denver. Today we find the loss of those historic sites unfortunate, but not because of the miners' success in finding gold. The Cherry Creek diggings amounted to a bust, turning the first nine months of the Pike's Peak rush into one of the western frontier's bigger fiascoes.

In its darkest hour, however, the Pike's Peak rush was redeemed by bonanza strikes in the gulches of the high mountains to the west. (Within fifteen years, dozens of mining districts and towns extended from the Cherry Creek diggings 150 miles southwest into the San Juans.) Miners turned steadily to rich lode deposits, developing hard-rock mines with legendary names like the London, Little Jonny, Smuggler-Union, Camp Bird and Sunnyside.

Of all Colorado gold discoveries, nothing before or after approached the fabulous strike at Cripple Creek, one of the world's greatest gold deposits, which bestowed upon Colorado a quarter century of prosperity and national prominence, helped establish the United States mint in Denver and, literally and figuratively, put the gold on the capitol dome.

Although after this bonanza, Colorado experienced no more gold rushes or Cripple Creeks, and Colorado's miners turned increasingly toward silver, lead, zinc and molybdenum, gold mining survived.

By the 1960s Colorado had produced over 40 million troy ounces of gold—nearly 1,400 standard tons—worth over $1 billion. But the richer ores were long gone, inflation had eroded the fixed price of the metal, and gold mining had nearly ceased. Gold mining in Colorado seemed about ready to join the narrow gauge railroads and the buffalo in the history books.

When "free market" gold emerged in the 1970s, the soaring prices brought back the miners and prospectors. They found new deposits, and many historic mines and districts found new life.

Today's modern mining methods and metallurgical extraction and recovery processes have allowed Colorado's annual gold output to enjoy a modest but sustained recovery. Colorado gold is also booming on the tourism and recreational fronts. Each year, tens of thousands of individuals tour old underground mines to touch veins of gold ore or try their luck at gold panning, hoping to wash out what may be the ultimate Colorado souvenir. And serious amateur miners, equipped with everything from the traditional gold pans to sophisticated dredges, still coax a little more gold out of the gravels once worked by the '59ers.

We can measure the legacy of Colorado gold in more than millions of troy ounces and billions of dollars. It also includes grand tales of fortunes made and fortunes lost, daring feats of exploration and mineral prospecting, technical achievements, intriguing legends of hidden mines and buried gold, quaint mountain towns and haunting ruins, and, perhaps most importantly, the promise of new bonanzas awaiting discovery in the canyons and gulches of the shining mountains.

Today, the allure of Colorado gold pulls as strongly as it did in 1859, when 100,000 gold seekers rushed for the "Pike's Peak country." This book gives the story of Colorado's part, past and present, in man's eternal search for gold.

—Lynda La Rocca

# ABOUT THE AUTHOR

Stephen M. Voynick has worked hardrock metal and placer gold deposits in Colorado, Wyoming, Arizona, Alaska, and Haiti. He knows about mining from personal experience and writes about it with great skill. With six books and hundreds of articles on mining-related topics to his credit, he serves also as a contributing editor to *Rock & Gem* magazine from his Leadville, Colorado, home.

*Colorado Gold: From Pikes Peak to the Present* is Voynick's third book from Mountain Press Publishing Company, following *Leadville: A Miner's Epic* (1984) and *Yogo: The Great American Sapphire* (1985). His earlier works are: *The Making of a Hardrock Miner* (Howell-North Books, 1978); *In Search of Gold* (Paladin Press, 1982); and *The Mid-Atlantic Treasure Coast* (Middle Atlantic Press, 1984). Voynick has recently completed a book-length manuscript detailing the History of Colorado's Climax Mine on commission for the Climax Molybdenum Company.

# INTRODUCTION

*There is a vein for the silver,*
*And a place for the gold where they refine it.*

Job 28 : 1

Those lines from the Old Testament, in their many interpretations, are often thought to be the origin of the familiar saying, "gold is where you find it." That expression, one of encouragement and untempered optimism, is what a prospector wants to believe—that the next pan of gravel or rock chip sample, from wherever it comes, will point the way to a nearby fortune in gold. During ancient times, prospectors doubtlessly thought that gold was "where you found it." But over the last century or two, geologists have shown us that gold occurs less capriciously. This knowledge gives those of us less versed in the intricacies of geology a simplified, yet valid, interpretation of the old saying: There are places where you can find gold, and there are places where you definitely won't find it.

Gold probably exists in the soil of your backyard, for the metal is widely distributed through the crust of the earth. Its average terrestrial abundance, however, is a mere 0.005 parts per million, which geologists call the normal geochemical background level. Extracting this gold makes little sense economically, for thousands of tons of earth contain but a single ounce of gold. When we speak of finding gold, we are actually referring to finding uncommon concentrations hundreds and even thousands of times higher than the terrestrial average. Like California and Alaska, Colorado has been blessed with many sites containing concentrations of gold, their origins all linked to the uplifting and volcanism that created the state's most prominent and celebrated topographical feature—the Rocky Mountains.

1

Some 300 million years ago tectonic stresses caused by the slow movement of massive portions of the earth's crust formed a geologically weakened zone across central and western Colorado. The stresses forced this zone to buckle upward, creating the Ancestral Rocky Mountains. Erosion eventually reduced the Ancestral Rockies to coarse gravels that formed the floors of broad valleys. Sixty-five million years ago, as the dinosaurs were approaching extinction in the semi-tropical climates of the late Cretaceous period, renewed tectonic stresses initiated another mountain-building episode. Great blocks of basement rock were forced upward to form the modern Rockies; although so high and massive that we would find them unrecognizable, this uplift created the primary ranges of central Colorado—the Front, Park and Sawatch. Tectonic stresses continued their effects, next causing a slow, more massive uplift, raising much of the southwestern United States, including Colorado, to its present elevation.

Both the mountain-building and regional uplifting caused severe faulting of the crust, creating deep fissures into which magma, or molten rock, surged upward from the depths. In southwestern Colorado, the magma often erupted onto the surface, solidifying into the massive volcanic formations we know as the San Juan Mountains. Volcanism occurred less frequently in central Colorado, where most of the magma was contained within crustal faults and fissures to form features geologists call intrusive bodies, including batholiths, stockworks, dikes and sills. Both the intrusions and volcanism fractured the surrounding country rock—the original geologic formations into which the intrusions moved—and were often associated with hydrothermal events, in which superheated mineral-bearing solutions are injected into the fractures. These solutions altered the rock and sometimes deposited minerals in bodies of widely varying composition and configuration. Most of this mineralization took place during the Tertiary period, about 20 to 40 million years ago.

Although erratic, mineralization occurred with particular frequency within a 150-mile-long, 30-mile-wide belt stretching diagonally from the present-day cities of Boulder, near the northern Front Range, to Durango, deep in the San Juans. This richly mineralized zone, which gained fame as the Colorado Mineral Belt, contained concentrated deposits of precious and base metals, notably gold, silver, lead, zinc, copper, tungsten and molybdenum.

Initially the gold occurred in lode deposits, that is, locked within solid rock either as nearly pure metal or as a telluride, a natural alloy of gold and tellurium, another metallic element. Sometimes the gold occurred in tiny microscopic particles dispersed through the rock. At other times the gold occurred as massive metal "stringers" in quartz veins, or even associated with other mineralization, including the sulfides of lead, zinc, silver and copper. Concentrations of gold varied from barely above the terrestrial average to rich veins and pockets containing tens and hundreds—and in rare instances even thousands—of ounces of gold per ton of "matrix", or surrounding rock.

Long before mineralization was completed, the mountains had been subjected to the continuous process of physical erosion and chemical weathering. Near the surface, sulfide mineralization oxidized, combining with the oxygen in the air to form materials that sometimes dissolved and were redeposited elsewhere, leaving behind gold in even further enriched concentrations.

Eventually, the surface rock was broken down by ice, water and wind into bits and pieces, freeing the contained gold. Water transported these alluvial gravels, sorting and resorting them by size and weight. Because of their great weight, the bits of gold that had been freed from their original lodes gradually became concentrated in the bottom layers of the alluvial gravel, forming placer deposits.

The final sculpting of the mountains and valleys into their present form occurred when a period of global cooling spawned the Pleistocene ice ages. Colorado was not swept by the great northern continental ice sheet, but by regional alpine glaciation over its higher elevations. Deep snowfall accumulated, compressing itself first into perpetual high snowfields, then into mobile glacial ice masses that scoured out and transported huge volumes of both solid rock and alluvial gravel. When temperatures moderated, the glaciers retreated, releasing enormous torrents of water that cut canyons and again resorted the glacial gravels, destroying many old gold placer deposits, while creating or enriching others. Most of gold placers that have been found in Colorado were formed during the retreat of the Pleistocene glaciers. Placer formation depended upon a complex combination of water volume and velocity, gradient, and the nature of the bedrock. In some locations, those conditions were nearly ideal to form gold placers of extraordinary richness.

Colorado gold, some of it in remarkably rich surface outcrops and some in bonanza concentrations in shallow placers, was now set for discovery.

*We hear nothing of gold, but much of disappointment,*
*suffering and repentance. Miners are leaving in crowds.*
*The speculation has exploded. Pike's Peak is no California.*

—The New York Times, May 18, 1859

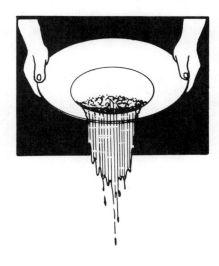

# 1

# PIKE'S PEAK OR BUST!
## 1858 – 1867

## The Bust

Who found the first Colorado gold, and where and when, is lost in prehistory. The gold may have been known to Indians, both the nomadic Utes, the hunters of the high mountains, and the Plains tribes that visited the mountain parks in summer. But the knowledge was apparently insignificant, for contrary to the colorful tales of "lost Indian mines", "golden ceremonial ornaments", and warriors who shot "golden rifle balls," these cultures had no interest in a metal too soft to fashion into tools or weapons.

The Spanish explorer Francisco Coronado passed very near the southeast corner of Colorado in his epic search for the mythical golden cities of Quivera in 1540-42. The Spanish, moving north from settlements at Santa Fe and Taos, did not venture into what is now Colorado until the 1600s. While no documentation confirms the discovery of gold, the Spanish did leave behind a host of intriguing gold-related legends and some physical evidence that, at the least, they prospected for the metal in the southern mountains. Some of these legends, including La Caverna del Oro—a "cave of gold" high in southern Colorado's Sangre de Cristo Range—survive even today, lending color and romance to the tales of early exploration.

By the mid-1700s French trappers had reached the eastern base of the Rockies by following most major rivers from Mexico to Canada. In 1758 Le Page du Pratz, in his *Histoire de la Louisiana*, told of a mine d'or, or gold mine, along the upper Arkansas River, describing "a rivulet whose waters rolled down gold dust." In 1804 Regis Loisel, a trader who had wandered west from St. Louis, told of "nuggets scattered here and there" on the upper Platte.

The first American to report the presence of gold in Colorado was James Purcell, a Kentucky-born adventurer, who reached the headwaters of the South Platte River in 1803. Purcell found placer gold and carried some in his shot pouch for months, only to discard it in a moment of desperation when he was certain he would never live to enjoy it. Several years later, Purcell reached the Spanish post of Santa Fe, where he reported his discovery to the U. S. Army explorer Zebulon Pike.

Reports of Colorado gold became increasingly frequent as more trappers and explorers made their way toward the shining mountains. In 1830 American trappers may have found gold on Clear Creek at the future site of Golden. In his *Commerce of the Prairies*, a classic account of trade along the Santa Fe Trail around 1840, Josiah Gregg told of a rich gold placer north of Taos and above the 37th parallel—the present Colorado-New Mexico line. When trapper-explorer Bill Williams returned to his Missouri home in 1841, he was said to have carried gold nuggets from the Colorado Rockies. And in 1848 members of Col. John Fremont's Army exploration party reportedly found gold near the present site of Lake City.

The discovery of the great California goldfields in 1848 dramatically dispelled any doubts about the existence of gold in the American West. Gold fever swept the nation, and thousands of '49s trekked overland to California along the established trails to the north and south of Colorado, steadfastly avoiding the rugged, unmapped and, to them, impenetrable Colorado Rockies.

Discoveries of Colorado gold significant enough to attract the attention of large numbers of people finally began in 1849. Army contractor George Simpson, exploring a creek whose bank was covered with a profusion of chokecherries (within the present city and county limits of Denver) panned about "25 cents worth of gold." A party of California-bound Cherokees, all with Georgia gold-mining experience, soon arrived, lured by the reports of gold on "Cherry Creek." They, too, found gold—enough to fill a goose quill—on a nearby tributary of Clear Creek, near the present site of Wadsworth Boulevard in Arvada. Their diary entries for June 20, 1850, include these simple notations: "Gold found," and "We called this Ralston's Creek because a man of that name found gold here." The party, led by Louis Ralston and John Beck, continued on to California, but other Cherokees and Georgians followed their footsteps to Colorado.

Reports continued to come out of the Rockies, including one of systematic mining of a placer deposit by soldiers stationed at Fort Massachusetts, in what is now northern Costilla County. Shortly after the post was established in 1852, gold was discovered at the nearby confluence of Grayback Gulch and Placer Creek. Soldiers pursued limited but apparently profitable mining until the army abandoned Fort Massachusetts in 1858.

In 1854 a portion of present-day Colorado became part of Kansas Territory giving businessmen in the eastern Kansas towns and posts near the Missouri River an added interest in the reports of gold. Should a gold rush ever develop, their towns would be the logical "jumping off" and outfitting points, promising them substantial financial benefits. As early as 1855, the Lawrence *Herald of Freedom* (Kansas Territory) printed reports of "gold in great abundance" near the headwaters of the Arkansas River.

By 1857 many of the Cherokees and Georgians who had visited Cherry Creek on their way to California had returned to their homes with western gold still on their minds. After planning a major prospecting expedition to Cherry Creek, two groups totalling 104 men—one group led by Georgia gold miner William Green Russell, the other by the 1850 Colorado visitors John Beck and Louis Ralston—met on the Great Plains at the Big Bend of the Arkansas in April 1858. By May they had arrived at the head of Cherry Creek, forty miles south of the future site of Denver, and quickly found traces of gold. Moving north, they camped at the confluence of Cherry Creek and the South Platte River (Confluence Park, near 16th Street and Interstate 25), then commenced prospecting creeks as distant as the Big Thompson River (near Loveland) without success. Discouragement set in quickly; by mid-June the party, now led by William Green Russell, numbered only thirteen. Those who had given up and left included Louis Ralston.

Meanwhile, a second group of prospectors arrived in the region. The Lawrence party, composed largely of men from Lawrence, had been lured by the stories of Fall Leaf, a Delaware Indian and army guide, who claimed to have found gold in 1857. The thirty-man Lawrence party headed for the region's most prominent landmark, Pike's Peak, but found no gold there, nor in South Park, and turned south into the San Luis Valley. At Fort Garland, which had just replaced old Fort Massachusetts, they heard exciting tales of another group under a William Green Russell of Georgia that had struck gold at Cherry Creek.

Russell's group had made their discovery on June 24, 1858, on the South Platte River, just over three miles upstream from the confluence of Cherry Creek (near the present Alameda Avenue bridge). One of Russell's close friends, James H. Pierce, later recounted the event:

> I discovered on the bank of the river a bed of alluvial gravel, and under it was a conglomerate or cement bedrock. I ran ahead to the wagons and got a pan, pick and shovel and had taken out a handful of gravel when Green Russell came up to me and finished washing it. We had about six or seven cents of nice scale gold. He then says in rather an excited tone: "Our fortune is made.". . .We panned several pans that evening and really the prospect was flattering. But it proved to be only a small deposit.
>
> We camped there for several days and made a hand rocker out of a cottonwood log and mined out something over $200 [about ten troy ounces] in thin scale gold.

Russell and another companion next prospected their way further up the South Platte River to the mouth of Little Dry Creek, then

*The confluence of Dry Creek and the South Platte River as it appears today. It is very near the site where the strike was made that started the Pike's Peak rush in 1858.*

moved about a mile up the gulch (near Broadway in present-day Englewood). Pierce continued:

> They got about $2.50 out of one panful of the dirt. We sank a hole four feet deep in the sand and got water to rock our dirt. We took out $50 in one day. That buoyed us up considerable...but this also proved, like our prospect on the Platte, but of little extent.

Word of the modest strike spread quickly along the Front Range, and the Lawrence party soon arrived from Fort Garland. So, too, did John Cantrell, who had heard the news at Fort Laramie and wanted to investigate before heading home to Westport (Kansas City). Russell gave Cantrell a sack full of the Dry Creek gravel to carry east. He reached Westport in August, where he panned the dirt before a public audience, then displayed the tiny, gleaming bits of gold. Kansas newspapers published front-page stories, along with Cantrell's affidavit stating that the dirt had come "from the Rocky Mountains and was just as it had come out of the mines."

Only days behind Cantrell were returning members of the Lawrence party. Although they apparently found nothing themselves, they eagerly reported the strike to their hometown friends—with a bit of embellishment. Details of the strike grew bigger day by day and were printed in *St. Louis Democrat* on September 10, 1858. On September 20 *The New York Times* reprinted the news on the front page:

### THE GOLD EXCITEMENT IN KANSAS

> Mr. E. Y. King arrived at Leavenworth City, on the 10th inst. [of this month], with a party from the Western Kansas Border. He left Cherry Creek, near Pike's Peak, on the 27th of July, having satisfactorily "prospected" a rich gold region extending from the tributaries of the South Platte to the headwaters of the Arkansas. . . . They join in the report that they found gold in all the places they "prospected," yielding from five to twenty-five cents to the panful of soil. It is in small particles, resembling the quartz soil washings of California.
>
> A company of 100 persons left Kansas City on Monday, the 13th inst., for the newly discovered gold region. . . .
>
> Thus it is rendered certain that the eastern as well as the western slope of the Rocky Mountains is richly treasured with gold. A new gold fever may be predicted as plainly at hand. . . .
>
> Within two weeks past, several persons have returned by different routes from the reported gold regions, all bringing with them the most enthusiastic report of the wealth of the Kansas "diggings," and what is better, specimens of the virgin ore. We have seen some specimens of a gold quartz which apparently

fully equals in value the richest ever brought from California. The fine gold, obtained from washing, is principally in the form of scales. This is in exceeding minute particles, and requires care, skill and proper implements to collect it thoroughly and successfully. Yet those who have worked diligently, have thus far realized, so say our informants, an average of TEN DOLLARS PER DAY.

We regard it now as a fixed FACT, beyond cavil or dispute, that we have in Kansas placers of gold equally as rich as those of California.

Eastern newspapers carried regular reports of the "Kansas gold fields," most reprinted verbatim from the Chicago and St. Louis dailies which, in turn, took their material straight from the Kansas newspapers. Unfortunately, the goal of the Kansas newspapers was to generate local economic development in eastern Kansas rather than to give factual reports of gold in western Kansas.

On September 28, 1858, Kansas gold again appeared on the front page of *The New York Times*, with its credibility this time linked directly to General James William Denver, Governor of Kansas Territory, but no better informed than anyone else:

LATEST BY TELEGRAPH FROM WASHINGTON
GOVERNOR DENVER ON THE KANSAS GOLD MINES

Governor Denver, writing to the Secretary of the Interior, September 17, says that the late news from Pike's Peak leaves no room to doubt the correctness of reported discoveries of gold in that vicinity. Prospectors have found gold on the Arkansas, on the heads of the Kansas, and on the South Fork of the Platte River, embracing an extent of country of more than three hundred miles. The richest mines are found on Cherry Creek, a tributary of the South Platte, directly north of Pike's Peak. Governor Denver has not yet heard of quartz veins, but the placer formation would seem to indicate a great similarity between these mines and the first discoveries in California.

In the public mind, Pike's Peak country had already become the "next California." In truth the "Kansas mines" were only holes dug in the gravels of the South Platte River bottom, most of which produced just that—gravel. The rumors of "quartz" gold were pure fabrications, aimed at creating another parallel with California which was by then turning toward lode mining of quartz veins in the Mother Lode. And the little gold that did come out of the South Platte gravels occurred only in the tiniest bits and flakes, not in California-sized gold nuggets. Nevertheless, on October 15, 1858 *The New York Times* offered this report on the "Kansas gold fields":

. . . Mr. Ben Clement will arrive here [Kansas City] in a few days with some $500 in gold, which he took out with nothing but camp tools and a pan; that with a rocker he could have done much better. Some of the men in company with Mr. Clement took out from twenty to one hundred and five dollars a day!

. . . picks and shovels were almost worth their weight in gold. So great was the excitement at Laramie that the Quartermaster was compelled to withhold the pay of those in the government employ in order to retain them. . . . He saw some of the finest specimens of quartz that probably have ever been found in a gold-bearing region, and one nugget of gold, weighing twenty-three ounces.

One of the few reports without at least one wild exaggeration ran in the *Lawrence Republican* on November 4, 1858. It leaves us with a fascinating picture of the Cherry Creek area before it became Denver:

. . . the general face of the country is rolling prairie, very sandy, supporting very little vegetation save the prickly pear. The bottoms, however, are very rich, and afford an abundance of pasture, the grass being from three to six feet high. The timber in the diggings is mainly cotton-wood, but within twenty miles are extensive pineries.

. . . The diggings are only ten miles from the base of the Rocky Mountains. Game is plenty in the vicinity of the diggings—such as antelope, black-tailed deer, Virginia deer, brown bears and "jack" rabbits. Grizzly bears are found in the mountains. . . . Wild ducks and geese are found on the river. The Platte at the diggings is about two hundred feet wide, easily fordable.

Those seeking to promote the gold rush picked a nearly perfect time to do it. In California, the wild excitement of 1849 had long faded, and thousands of restless miners milled about waiting impatiently for the "next California." In the East, the financial Panic of 1857, a prolonged drought that ruined many farmers, and the uncertainties generated by an impending Civil War had created economic depression and rampant unemployment. Many United States citizens were eager for another major Western gold rush.

Would-be developers were already laying out two town sites, Auraria and Denver, when the first wave of gold seekers arrived at Cherry Creek in the fall of 1858. Many more were heading for the Missouri River towns in eastern Kansas Territory to outfit and await spring before pushing west across the Plains. The river towns boomed; merchants and traders were hard-pressed to keep up with demand for horses, mules, oxen, wagons, tents, mining equipment, and general supplies and provisions, as newspapers continued reporting more gold than ever coming out of the "Kansas mines."

On Cherry Creek, two of William Green Russell's brothers had departed for Georgia, taking with them all the gold their party had mined during 1858. The gold was believed sold to the United States Mint at Dahlonega, Georgia, and coined. The first significant quantity of gold known to have been mined in Colorado met a fitting end, considering the role Georgians played in its discovery. However, in five months, the Russell party had mined only about forty ounces of gold worth perhaps eight hundred dollars—hardly the stuff of which "Californias" were made. No one realized that fact better than James Pierce, who, with the ten remaining members of the Russell party, had settled into crude cabins along Cherry Creek to wait out the winter. The only "mining" still underway was some pick-and-shovel work on Dry Creek, and Pierce was astounded to see the early arrivals begin pouring in from the Missouri River.

> By Christmas there must have been a thousand men on the South Platte. . . . As yet nothing worthy of excitement had even been found, nothing but some little deposits near the Platte and the light float gold on Cherry Creek and a little bar on Ralston and gold on Clear Creek—these were all that had been found up to that time.
>
> The emigrants, having gotten here too late to prospect for themselves, were disposed to discredit what we told them and believed we really had a big bonanza awaiting the return of our comrades in the spring of 1859. So many of them sat in their cabins writing big yarns, and many of them drawing largely on their prolific brains and writing back for truth what was nothing but a hallucination of the brain. By this time, all had gone into town site speculations. . . . Before spring there were perhaps twenty cities in this country as large as New York, minus the wealth, population and buildings. That is, they had the ground to build on, but nothing to build with.
>
> . . . It is now February, and men are spending their time in hunting and prospecting a little, but nothing is discovered to justify all this town business. What was to support it all? No mines that would pay wages. Thousands of men back on the Missouri waiting for the ice to give way so they could come to the great bonanza at Pikes Peak, as all the eastern newspapers called it.

By early spring of 1859 both the tone and content of the newspaper reports changed. Gone were the tales of 23-ounce nuggets, men washing out $100 per day, and quartz gold rivaling the best in California. In their place appeared reports of the building excitement in the Missouri River towns of eastern Kansas Territory, confusing tales of "partial confirmation" of earlier discoveries, and even occasional mention of destitute, half-starved individuals straggling back east across the Plains claiming that the whole thing was a cruel hoax.

But these doubts failed to head off the great Pike's Peak gold rush. It began in earnest in February 1859, at the first hint of spring, when thousands, then tens of thousands, headed out onto the Plains. They walked, rode, pulled their own carts; the most fortunate had ox-drawn wagons, the canvas emblazoned with words destined to be a colorful part of frontier history: PIKE'S PEAK OR BUST.

The Pike's Peak gold rush was nearly at its peak when *The New York Times* shocked its readers on May 18, 1859:

### THE PIKES PEAK DELUSION

The reports from the new mining region, which, until lately, have been contradictory, are now set with steady current in one direction. We hear nothing of gold, but much disappointment, suffering and repentance. Miners are leaving in crowds. Pike's Peak is no California. Its gold is scarce; its climate inhospitable; its discouragement manifold. Famine, that grim visitor, is there, and deaths have occurred from starvation.

This emigration to the supposed mines has been very large, especially from the western United States—a great proportion of the young men of the Mississippi Valley having left their homes for the diggings early in the Spring. The loss and suffering incurred must be enormous. They will return, some of them as can, stripped of everything, to begin again the labors from which visions of gold allured them.

Spring 1859 was a time of terrible confusion, disappointment and bitterness in Denver City, the newly named town at the confluence of the South Platte River and Cherry Creek. As the wide-eyed newcomers arrived they passed the long lines of "go-backers," those who had arrived early only to spend a long, hungry winter on Cherry Creek. When the new arrivals learned that the "Kansas mines" were no California, some turned around the next day and, short on food and supplies, headed back east across the Plains, decrying the "Pike's Peak Hoax." On May 25, 1859, *The New York Times* told how the Pike's Peak rush had turned not only to bust, but to tragedy, reporting examples of extreme hardship:

### DEPLORABLE ACCOUNTS FROM THE PIKE'S PEAK EMIGRANTS

#### STARVATION AND DEATH——DEAD BODIES DEVOURED

The regular correspondent of the [St. Louis] Democrat writing from Denver City on the 9th inst., recounts a most deplorable

*Ruins of the Fanny Rawlings Mine at Leadville. The Fanny Rawlings was one of Leadville's big gold producers at the turn of the century.*

condition of things on the Plains. Many of the emigrants were dying of starvation, while others were subsisting on prickly pears and wild onions found along the road. The stage agent reports picking up a man named Blue, who was reduced to a skeleton from starvation. He had started with his two brothers. One of them died, and the remaining two ate his body. A man named Gibbs had reached the mines in starving condition, and expressed the opinion that his party, numbering nine, had all perished. Many graves are reported along the route, and much property has been abandoned and destroyed along the road.

The nation, which only months earlier had thrilled to the reports of the "great discoveries" being made daily in the "Kansas goldfields," now learned that the Pike's Peak rush was the Pike's Peak bust.

# The Boom

*If I only had a pick and a pan instead of a hunting knife and cup, I could dig out a sack full of the yellow stuff . . .*

George A. Jackson, January 7, 1859
at the future site of Idaho Springs

In one of the frontier's great ironies, the Pike's Peak rush at its darkest hour had already been redeemed. In early May 1859, just as the eastern newspapers were proclaiming the doom of the Pike's Peak rush, George A. Jackson and a few partners walked into a general store in Denver City and placed 100 ounces of raw placer gold upon the rough wooden counter. Worth about $1,900, it probably equalled all the gold mined at Cherry Creek during the past year. But Jackson and his partners had washed their 100 ounces of gold out of the South Fork of Clear Creek in just seven days. Furthermore, Jackson had made his discovery four months earlier, in January 1859.

George Jackson was no stranger to the West, nor to gold, having learned his prospecting skills in California, and later working as a hunter, trapper and army guide. Passing by Cherry Creek in July 1858, Jackson learned of the gold mined by the Russell party and stayed on. He prospected Ralston Creek with no luck, then moved into a winter cabin below Table Mountain near the present site of Golden.

15

On the last day of 1858 Jackson headed west into Clear Creek Canyon on a hunting trip. After shooting an elk, his companions packed the meat back, but Jackson continued on alone through deep snow, exploring his way up the South Fork of Clear Creek to the present site of Idaho Springs. He camped near hot springs where he saw "hundreds of beautiful mountain sheep, great bucks with curled horns, all grazing about the springs where the warm vapors had melted the snow and left the grass for them to nibble at." Jackson shot one for meat for himself and his dogs, then moved a few hundred yards up a tributary to prospect. He built a roaring bonfire to thaw a promising-looking gravel bar, scraped out some of the gravel, then panned it in his tin drinking cup. Encouraged by a few flakes of gold,

*An undisturbed section of Clear Creek Canyon, just west of Denver. This was the route taken by many hopeful prospectors and miners to reach the great 1859 gold strikes at Idaho Springs and Central City.*

he continued digging with his knife and washing the dirt in his cup. After several hours he had recovered a small nugget and one ounce of gold in bits and flakes—spectacular results for washing so little gravel. That night, January 7, 1859, Jackson huddled by his camp fire and recorded in his journal the elation that follows a major gold discovery, which few prospectors ever experience:

> I jumped up and down and told myself the story I would tell . . . when I got back to our camp under Table Mountain. After a good supper of meat—bread and coffee all gone—I went to bed and dreamed of riches galore in that bar. If I only had a pick and a pan instead of a hunting knife and the cup, I could dig out a sack full of the yellow stuff and carry it down to the boys. My mind ran upon it all night long. I dreamed all sorts of things— about a fine house and good clothes, a carriage and horses, travel, what I would take to the folks down in old Missouri and everything you can think of—I had struck it rich!

While almost all prospectors would have experienced a similar elation, very few would have done what Jackson did next. He did not rush into Denver City wild-eyed and bragging about his strike. Instead he told only a few trusted partners; then, to earn "a few dollars" and bide his time for a few months, he did some casual trading as far north as Fort Laramie. And on his return to Denver City, he watched the bitterly disappointed "go-backers" leaving for the East. Finally, in April, he assembled a small group of backers from Chicago, outfitted, and guided them back up the South Fork of Clear Creek. The going was so rough that they dismantled the wagons and carried them in pieces up the rugged canyon. They arrived at Jackson's strike, now named Chicago Creek, on May 6, 1859. Again they took the wagons apart, reassembling the planks as sluice boxes that washed out $1,900 of gold in just one week.

"Jackson's Diggings" alone could have saved the Pike's Peak rush. But just as production mining started on Chicago Creek, another prospector, John Gregory, struck it rich on the North Fork of Clear Creek—not far from Jackson's Diggings, but separated by a 10,000-foot-high ridge. John Gregory, an Alabama-born mule skinner, had learned about gold in Dahlonega, Georgia. While passing through Fort Laramie in the early spring of 1859, Gregory decided to investigate Cherry Creek. By early May he had panned his way down the Front Range creeks to Denver City without luck. Grubstaked by an Indiana party, Gregory then turned his attention to Clear Creek, panning his way a few miles up the North Fork. Following a trail of color a half mile up a small gulch, he found a weathered, heavily-stained outcrop of "rotten" quartz. He filled a pan with the crumbling

*The north wall of Gregory Gulch near Black Hawk as it appears today. The original vertical vein outcrop of gold-bearing quartz (center, top to bottom) has been completely mined out. This was one of the outcrops discovered in 1859.*

quartz and, even without crushing it, washed out a quarter-ounce of gold worth over four dollars.

The outcrop was an oxidized vein of rich gold-bearing quartz feeding the placer below, in what would soon be named Gregory Gulch, with bits of free gold. Although the surface of the outcrop had completely crumbled, the quartz beneath, while oxidized, was still a durable rock that the miners had to hammer to pieces to free the contained gold. The hammering was well worth their effort though, for single pans yielded as much as $10 in gold; in one case, four days of work on a 100-foot-long claim rewarded four miners with $972. John Gregory himself worked only a short time crushing and washing quartz. He sold his two discovery claims for $21,000, then sold his services and reputation as a master prospector to others for the then unheard of fee of $200 per day.

At about the same time as Jackson's and Gregory's strikes, gold was discovered along upper Boulder Creek, near the present site of Nederland. The first strike, at the junction of South Boulder and Beaver Creeks, was called the Deadwood Diggings; a second rich placer was discovered six miles to the northeast on Gold Run. Word of the "honest" strikes galvanized Denver City. Town-site promoters and merchants were said to have fallen to their knees, shouting, "Thank God, the country's saved!" For a while, that exclamation seemed a paradox, for the residents of Denver City, the surrounding town sites and the Cherry Creek diggings left them nearly abandoned in their rush for the mountains.

Convincing the nation that, this time, gold indeed awaited prospectors in the Pike's Peak country took time. Most newspapers were now wary of printing wild rumors and waited for solid evidence—gold itself. It was June 28, 1859, before *The New York Times* again reversed its stand and declared the Pike's Peak gold rush real:

THE PIKE'S PEAK GOLD
. . . From the [Leavenworth] Times we learned that the Pikes Peak Express reached Leavenworth on the 20th [June], in eight days from Denver City, bringing in $2,500 in dust on consignment. . . .
First, placers of coarse gold, decomposed and gold-bearing quartz have been discovered in the mountains and are now being successfully worked. Second, if a result of $20 to $100 per diem to the man may be accepted as "paying quantities," then these mines are eminently practicable. As to the gold, since the whole country is clamorous to see it, and it must be conceded as essential to reviving our faith in Pike's Peak . . . It was computed that there was already $25,000 in dust at Denver City, but there was no specie nor provisions to purchase it with, but as both have in all probability since arrived there, it is not improbable that large receipts will be announced by the incoming Express.

The gold arrived by stagecoach in the Missouri River towns, first by the hundreds of ounces, then by the thousands, and the second phase of the Pike's Peak rush began. Throughout the summer of 1859 newcomers arrived in Denver City at the rate of well over a hundred per day. The posts along the Smoky Hill Trail in Kansas reported "thousands of wagons" passing by. The Platte River Route, connecting Denver City with the Overland Trail in Nebraska, observers described as "having but a single train" that extended all the way from the shining mountains to the Missouri River, taking six weeks to pass.

19

*Central City as it appears today. Central City was Colorado's first true gold camp of the Pike's Peak rush.*

By June prospectors had claimed virtually every foot of the three-mile-long Gregory Gulch and its gold-bearing tributaries. At a time when United States wage earners averaged about $500 per year, miners lucky enough to stake a good 100-foot-long claim on Gregory Gulch were averaging about $50 per day. While some worked with nothing but pans, most shoveled gravel and crudely crushed quartz into heavy wooden sluice boxes. Over 5,000 people crowded into Gregory Gulch; dozens of camps sprang nearby, and the centrally located collection of shacks and tents at the junction of Gregory and Nevada gulches became Central City.

William Green Russell shared in the bonanza, putting his name on a rich gulch just south of Gregory Gulch. In June, six miners working two, 100-foot-long claims in Russell Gulch washed out $1,200 in one week. Two months later, 900 men were working the entire length of Russell Gulch, taking out about $35,000 in gold each week.

To more thoroughly and quickly crush the quartz ores, miners first turned to *arrastres*, circular depressions in bedrock around which mules pulled heavy grinding boulders. Grinding became even more efficient when the first of many steam-powered stamp mills went into operation in Gregory Gulch in September. The stamp mills employed cast-iron stamps weighing as much as one ton each. The bigger mills

20

had a dozen stamps lifted rhythmically by a large concentric cam-shaft, then allowed to drop onto the quartz ores passing beneath them. The crushed ores were washed in sluices equipped with mercury-filled riffles, recovering even the finest particles of free "flour" gold by amalgamation. However, overall gold recovery was still terribly inefficient. The coarse crushing in the pounding stamp mills left much of the gold still contained in quartz, which washed right over the mercury riffles and out of the sluice boxes. The miners were losing about half of the gold, yet, interestingly, it was of little concern to them. Some of the vein outcrops were so rich—over ten ounces of gold per ton—that loss of half of it made little difference in the miners' short term perspective of that first hectic summer. Miners made fortunes not by recovery efficiency, but by the sheer volume of ore they put through coarse crushing and quick washing.

*Partially restored stamp mill. Powered by steam, the cams lifted heavy rods and stamps to crush the ore below.*

Chicago Creek, Gold Run and Gregory and Russell gulches formed only the beginning. Prospectors found gold further up the South Fork of Clear Creek all the way to Empire and Georgetown. Prospectors made bigger strikes in South Park in July, when they found gold along a dozen tributaries of Tarryall Creek and the upper South Platte River. Camps with names including Montgomery, Buckskin Joe, Sterling City, Tarryall, Hamilton, Park City and Fairplay sprang up almost overnight.

By August, prospectors had moved north from Tarryall, crossed the Continental Divide over Georgia Pass, descended into the Blue River drainage and made another spectacular series of placer strikes at Gold Run (one of four "Gold Runs" in Colorado), Georgia, American, French and Humbug gulches, the Swan River, and on the main channel of the Blue River itself. Some of these strikes were "pound diggings," where one man could wash out a pound of gold every day. The Weaver brothers, discoverers of Gold Run, took out 96 pounds of gold—well over 1,000 ounces—in just six weeks. Of the host of new camps that appeared, Breckenridge, at the confluence of French Gulch and the Blue River, became the district seat.

Most mining stopped in October, with the onset of the long and bitter high-country winter. A few stubborn miners kept at it, however, determined to make their fortunes before an even bigger horde of prospectors surged through the mountains in spring. In Nevada Gulch, a mile above Central City, a solitary miner began rocking some rich dirt in November. By January, he had taken out 150 ounces of gold worth about $2,600.

The 1859 gold production may have been as high as 50,000 ounces, worth nearly $900,000. Pike's Peak country suddenly became an important producer of gold with the promise of far more to come. And with a population of perhaps 50,000, political organization became both a local and federal priority. Both Kansas and Nebraska territories had loose claims to the region, but their capitols were too far east to effectively govern the area around Denver City. But what concerned legislators the most, as civil war drew near in the East, was the political division among the gold seekers themselves. Southerners had made most of the big strikes, and some voices in the South were already proclaiming a "right of discovery." The region's complex geographical-political picture further confused the question. To the west, Utah was a "maverick" territory, with no particular allegiance to the North or the South. Strong Southern sympathies, however, existed in the territories of Kansas and New Mexico, and the state of Texas, only five hundred miles from Denver, was already a pillar of the emerging Confederacy. Yet most of the population of the Pike's Peak country, as well as the limited investment capital that had arrived, came from the North.

Since those who had established the mountain mining districts were accustomed to solving their own problems, they established their own territory in the fall of 1859, named it Jefferson, and petitioned Congress for immediate admission to the Union as a state. Congress rejected the petition on two counts: First, the federal legislators refused to deal with a "self-appointed" territory; second, admitting an ostensibly Northern state, when the last desperate efforts were underway to preserve the Union, they found politically unacceptable. The Pike's Peak country remained loosely organized as Jefferson Territory for well over a year.

Spring 1860 brought increased gold production from more systematic mining as well as an exciting string of new strikes. Prospectors had reached the upper Arkansas River in fall 1859, finding color in the main channel and tributaries, including Cache Creek and Lake Creek. Returning in April, they moved north toward the present site of Leadville, then panned their way six miles up a gulch to make the richest placer strike of the entire Pike's Peak rush. California Gulch, so named because it seemed to have "all the gold of Californy," soon filled with thousands of people and new camp, Oro City, which, of course, was a "city" in name only. The new arrivals included Webster D. Anthony, who recorded this impression in his journal:

> Wednesday, July 18th, 1860 . . . Was surprised at seeing so large a town, where only a few weeks ago not a house was seen, and not a wagon ever made its track. Now the crooked street on both sides is walled up with log Palaces, and at least 8,000 inhabitants claim this as their Mountain home until fortune favors them and their Purses become fat with the "filthy Lucre," the "Root of all Evil." Such is the rush for these mines when a new Gulch is discovered.
>
> The streets appear as though everyone built his cabin in its own place without regard to survey and as a consequence they are very crooked. The mining portion of the Gulch is about six miles long and nearly every claim is being worked and at the store the sound of gravel and shovel is heard as they "wash out" with their "Toms." Have heard much about the population and rapid growth of these "fast cities" but to appreciate them one must see for themselves. From the appearance should think that gamblers ruled the place, from the numerous "Hells" which they have erected. And from the general inhabitants of young "Oro" should judge they would hardly rank among first society.

"First society" or not, miners found an enormous amount of the "filthy lucre" waiting in the gravels of California Gulch. They staked virtually its entire seven-mile length into 339 hundred-foot-long claims. Some of the best of these claims paid $65,000 in their first season. Three miners who chanced into a "glory hole," a rich pocket on bedrock, washed out $216 in two hours. Four others, through both mining and speculating on claims, walked away from California Gulch with $100,000 each after that first glorious season of 1860.

In the continuing quest for more pound diggings prospectors from Breckenridge moved west across the Mosquito Range, while California Gulch men followed the Arkansas River north to its headwaters and crossed over Fremont Pass. Arriving on the headwaters of Tenmile Creek, they struck gold on McNulty Gulch. Although small in size, McNulty Gulch may have had the highest grade of gravel of the rush. At one choice location, several square yards of exposed bedrock produced $3,000. Some individual pans yielded as much as $100, or about six ounces of raw placer gold.

Gold production in 1860 was an estimated 125,000 ounces—about four standard tons—worth over $2 million. The miners produced almost all of it by "shovel-in" sluice-box washing of either crudely crushed quartz ores or placer gravels. Accurately determining how much gold was produced was impossible, however. The region lacked both a central place for miners to sell their gold, and enough gold or silver specie for which miners preferred to exchange it. Since merchants had little confidence in the wildly fluctuating government "greenbacks," they took raw placer gold—"dust"—in trade, and claim owners paid wages in dust. Newly mined gold immediately became a circulating medium of exchange, and accounting for it became impossible.

The indeterminate dollar value of raw gold also created problems, especially for miners trying to sell their gold. The price of fine, or pure, gold was fixed by the United States government at $20.67 per troy ounce. But gold never occurs pure; instead, it is always alloyed with other metals, mostly silver. South Platte River gold was the purest in the region, about 950 fine, or 95 percent pure, and could be exchanged for $20 in coin or merchandise. Most gold from the mountain gulches, however, was 800 to 880 fine, and worth a lower equivalent in coin. In trade, merchants had an advantage. Miners needing provisions had no choice but to take the prevailing "exchange," a rate which merchants as distant as Omaha tried to keep at $14 per troy ounce, and sometimes as low as $10. "Dealing dust" was a practice fraught with trickery and risk. Gold buyers, usually merchants and brokers, often used scales weighted in their favor. But

*The Clark, Gruber & Co. mint building shortly after it was built in Denver in 1860. At the time it was the most impressive building in Denver.*

sometimes the gold they bought had enough brass and bronze shavings in it to more than make up the difference.

The miners' only other option to sell their gold was to consign it to a broker or express company, taking a paper receipt. The gold was shipped east by stage to the Missouri River towns, then on to St. Louis where it was transshipped by rail, sometimes as far as the Philadelphia Mint for assaying and purchase with payment in coin. Two months later, coin or a check would arrive, minus brokerage, assaying and shipping fees, as well as a steep insurance premium amounting to as much as five percent of gross value both ways. One ounce of gulch dust containing $17.50 worth of fine gold might return only about $13 after a long wait. In one of the ironies of Jefferson Territory gold-rush economics, brokers sometimes lacked sufficient coin to cover the check when it finally arrived, leaving some frustrated, angry miners to take "payment" in someone else's raw placer gold.

Formal banking and assaying in Jefferson Territory began with Clark, Gruber & Co., founded in 1858 as a brokerage house in Leavenworth by Austin M. and Milton E. Clark, from Ohio, and Emanuel Henry Gruber, of Maryland. Initially, the company took receipt of small amounts of dust as it arrived in Leavenworth, then quickly established an office in Denver after news of the Jackson and Gregory strikes. Although business boomed, Clark, Gruber & Co. faced several problems, with as much as $300,000 tied up in transit, and being itself burdened by high shipping and insurance rates. The best solution appeared to them to be establishing a private mint. At the time, the United States had no laws to the contrary, requiring only that the private coinage be of "full weight."

Milton Clark purchased the necessary dies and equipment in Philadelphia, shipped everything west by rail to St. Louis then by ox-drawn freight wagons to Denver. It arrived in April 1860; by July Clark, Gruber & Co. had the assaying and minting equipment ready for operation in a new two-story brick building near the center of rapidly growing Denver. The company extended invitations to leading citizens, including William Byers, editor and publisher of the fledgling *Rocky Mountain News*, to witness the minting of the first "Pike's Peak" gold coins. Byers reported the event on July 25, 1860:

> In compliance with which invitation we forthwith repaired to the elegant banking house of [Clark, Gruber & Co.] on the corner of [present Market and 16th Streets], and were admitted to their coining room in the basement, where we found preparations almost complete for the issue of Pike's Peak coin. A hundred "blanks" had been prepared, weight and fineness tested and last manipulations gone through with, prior to their passage through the stamping press. The little engine that drives the machinery was fired up, belts adjusted, and between three and four o'clock the machinery was put in motion and "mint drops" of the value of $10 each began dropping into a tin pail with the most musical "chink." About a thousand dollars were turned out at the rate of fifteen or twenty coins a minute, which were deemed very satisfactory for the first experiment.
>
> The coins—of which none but ten dollar pieces are yet coined—are seventeen grains heavier than the U.S. coin of the same denomination.
>
> On the face is a representation of the peak, its base surrounded by a forest of timber, and "Pikes Peak Gold" encircling the summit. Immediately under its base is the word "Denver," and beneath it "Ten D.". On the reverse is the American Eagle,

encircled by the name of the firm "Clark, Gruber & Co." and beneath the date, "1860."

The coin . . . is upon the whole, very creditable in appearance, and a vast improvement over "dust" as a circulating medium.

The $10 gold coin was soon joined by a $20 coin of similar design. Clark, Gruber & Co. posted flyers around town and in some of the mountain mining camps, and the *Rocky Mountain News* began running their advertisements on August 8, 1860:

We have in connection with our banking house a MINT, and are prepared to exchange our coin for gold dust. The native gold is coined as it is found alloyed with silver. The weight will be greater, but the value the same as the United States coin of like denomination.

Clark, Gruber & Co. was soon minting $18,000 in gold coins each week, including new denominations of $5 and $2.50 gold coins similar in design to U.S. Mint issues. The obverse bore the head of the Goddess of Liberty surrounded by thirteen stars, with "Clark & Company" filling the tiara. On the reverse was an eagle encircled by "Pike's Peak Gold, Denver," followed by "5 D." or "2 ½ D." The coins were 825 fine, that is, they contained 82.5 percent pure gold, with the remainder silver. They also weighed slightly more than corresponding U.S. Mint issues, but contained exactly the same amount of gold. The additional silver present actually made them worth one-half percent more than U.S. Mint gold coins.

The private coinage of Clark, Gruber & Co. helped stabilize the regional economy and keep more of the territory's gold at home, at a time when Jefferson Territory needed all the help it could get. Southern secession began late in 1860, making civil war all but inevitable. Only then did Congress authorize establishment of Colorado Territory, effective February 22, 1861. When war erupted in April, Colorado Territory soon felt the effects. Communications and transportation channels were disrupted, immigration slowed to a trickle, and the arrival of outside investment capital almost stopped. Withdrawals of federal troops from the West left the territory increasingly vulnerable to both Indian trouble and Southern guerilla activity.

To allay fears, discourage shipment of guns or gold to the South, and assure that Colorado Territory would remain solidly with the North, Governor William Gilpin organized two volunteer infantry regiments. When Washington refused to back an unauthorized territorial militia, Gilpin outfitted his troops with funds raised from equally unauthorized drafts on the federal treasury. Although controversial, the Colorado Volunteers provided the territory with a calming military presence at a time when Southern threats, both real and imagined, ranged from attacks on the mines to taking over the Clark, Gruber & Co. mint. The Colorado Volunteers would later distinguish themselves in a series of actions at La Glorieta Pass in New Mexico, helping eliminate the threat of "invasion" by Southern units from Texas.

Washington reacted with increasing concern over the "private armies" and "private mints" of Colorado; the Treasury Department believed that issuing coinage, especially in a sparsely populated, infant territory, would be better handled by the federal government. Since the slightest impropriety could create trouble with Washington, Clark, Gruber & Co. maintained a policy of absolute honesty in all its business, even altering its coinage in 1861. The new Pike's Peak gold coins were given one percent more gold than U.S. Mint issues to "protect the holder against loss by wear," but more likely to protect Clark, Gruber & Co. against any question of full weight. Even the designs were changed; although the coins still bore "Pike's Peak" and "Clark, Gruber & Co.," they were altered to more closely resemble U.S. Mint issues.

Two other, smaller private mints were established in 1861. John Parson & Co. founded their mint in the South Park camp of Hamilton, while J. J. Conway & Co. began buying, assaying and minting gold coins in Georgia Gulch, near Breckenridge. The Parson coins looked similar to U.S. Mint issues, but the Conway coins had a simpler design. Both, however, bore the name of "Pike's Peak."

In 1861 Colorado produced about 150,000 ounces of gold worth over $2.5 million, and Clark, Gruber & Co. minted a half million dollars in coins. Noting the increasing gold production and coinage, the Treasury Department proposed establishing a United States Branch Mint at Denver to "properly regulate" gold purchasing and coinage, and perhaps to discourage the suspected flow of gold going to the South.

A second proposal called for the immediate prohibition of private coinage in the United States. The bill to establish the Denver Branch Mint to purchase and assay but not coin gold was introduced into Congress in December 1861. When territory residents began to doubt the financial ability of the federal government to purchase the Clark, Gruber & Co. mint, a territory-wide, grassroots movement grew to keep the private facility in operation.

In 1862 Colorado's gold production soared to an estimated 225,000 troy ounces—over seven standard tons—worth about $4 million. Largely because of the record production, Congress authorized the

Treasury Department to purchase the building and mint equipment of Clark, Gruber & Co.; the private mint stopped purchasing gold and all coinage operations ceased late in 1862, pending final transfer to the federal government the following April. During its two and one-half years of operation as a private mint, Clark, Gruber & Co. coined $594,305 in Pike's Peak gold and purchased another 77,000 troy ounces of raw gold worth $1.4 million. Not included in those figures were large amounts of dust shipped on consignment to the U.S. Mint at Philadelphia. Clark, Gruber & Co. remained in the banking business until 1865, when its assets were absorbed into the First National Bank of Denver.

While the Civil War raged, the nation's newspapers were filled primarily with news of military actions and political issues. After a two-year absence from the pages of *The New York Times*, news of Colorado gold reappeared on January 6, 1863, with an article reflecting the national economic importance of the territory's mine production.

### GOLD FROM COLORADO

Probably half the people of New York are yet unaware that there is a political territorial organization in the United States called Colorado, which is rapidly rising to the proportions of a State, and is even now contributing largely to the national wealth . . .

The actual amount of gold taken from the soil of Colorado during the year just gone by, reaches a value of about six million dollars; an agent of the government who has just returned from an inspection of the mining operations, states that the mines now being worked will produce during the current year over twelve million dollars worth of gold. There are now 30,000 inhabitants in the territory, and the extraordinary prosperity it is enjoying is attracting both capital and immigration. The effects of the war are felt little out there, and such questions as rich leads, big strikes and contested claims cause more excitement than the great battles of which they hear from the States.

. . . The amount of gold which we received from California during the last year was nearly ten million less than in 1861, and if we do not capture or sink the Alabama [the Confederate warship harassing merchant shipping], it will probably be very far short this year. But our supplies from Colorado, which will come overland, will probably make up the deficit.

While a secure supply of Colorado gold was important to the North, the projections of ever higher production were wishful thinking. Colorado's gold miners enjoyed two more $4 million years in 1863 and 1864, but the Pike's Peak boom was about over. The last major placer strikes came in 1860. Placer gold was found in Washington Gulch in Gunnison County in 1861, on Colorado Gulch in Lake County in 1863, and again near Hahn's Peak in Routt County in 1864, but none of these finds approached the richness of the earlier strikes.

The heyday of the independent placer miner had also passed. Not only had the bonanza gravels been depleted, but water had become an expensive commodity. Diverted water was an absolute necessity to placer mining, but only affluent companies could dig the ten- and fifteen-mile-long diversion ditches to supply it. Since few independent miners could afford to pay for their water while mining lower grade gravels, their only alternative was to consolidate claim ownership, often under the names of the growing number of ditch companies. In the great days of 1859 most of Colorado's placer miners were independents; by 1861 most were paid day laborers working another man's, or a company's, consolidated claims.

Lode mining was also running into trouble, for the spectacular outcrops of "picture rock"—quartz carrying ten or twenty ounces of gold per ton—were becoming hard to find. Miners could no longer afford inefficient recovery of gold in lower grade ores. But lode mining's biggest problem was that the miners had nearly worked out shallow, oxidized portions of the rich vein outcrops. At depths of only thirty or forty feet, miners encountered sulfide mineralization. Although an enormous amount of gold was left in the non-oxidized ore, it was intimately associated with silver and base-metal sulfides which dramatically reduced the miners' ability to recover the gold by amalgamation. Since 1861 miners had tried to deal with these refractory—literally, "stubborn"—ores with techniques ranging from improved crushing to roasting and the use of steam and chemicals, all without success. By 1864 as much as 75 percent of the gold contained in the refractory ores was lost in the tailings, and lode mining around Central City was about to stop.

In 1865 the year the Civil War ended, Colorado's gold production dropped to $3 million dollars. And in 1866 and 1867 it dropped below $2 million, or about 110,000 ounces of gold each year. By that time, almost ten years after William Green Russell's discovery of gold on Dry Creek, Colorado's cumulative gold production was estimated at about 1.25 million ounces—forty standard tons—of gold worth at least $25 million. Sixty percent of that bonanza was placer gold, making 1858-1867 the only period in Colorado's mining history in which placer production ever exceeded, or even approached, the output of the lode gold mines.

In terms of gold production, Colorado never became the "next California." California, in its first decade of mining, had produced at least $400 million in gold—sixteen times more than that mined in Colorado. Nevertheless, the forty tons of gold taken from the placers and outcrops of Colorado had created a territory, populated a wilderness and helped sustain faith in the West. Perhaps most importantly, those forty tons of Pike's Peak gold merely hinted at the mineral treasures that still waited in the shining mountains. In the decades that followed, Colorado's prospectors made strikes against which all the gold mined during the ten years that followed the Pike's Peak rush paled in comparison.

*Gold has been called the first folly of man, the whore of civilization, a barbarous relic, the savior of civilization, and host of other fanciful, if at times derogatory, epithets. Nevertheless, man has retained a curious fascination for the metal for over 5,000 years.*

—Robert W. Boyle, *Gold: History and Genesis of Deposits*

# 2

# A MOST REMARKABLE METAL

In 1859, 100,000 people, many acting on rumor alone, rushed for the unknown Pike's Peak country. Just as in the earlier California gold rush, nothing but gold could have inspired such a migration. California, of course, wasn't the first gold rush, and Colorado wasn't the last. Over the thousands of years since early man first collected and became enamored of the yellow metal, gold has profoundly influenced our history. That any inanimate material could exert such a powerful, however irrational, attraction for people reflects gold's many remarkable and unique properties.

Gold, while certainly uncommon, is not the rarest of metals, ranking 58th in abundance among the 92 natural elements. Gold has an atomic weight of 197, a relative measurement of the mass of elements. Only a handful of elements have greater mass, including uranium (238), bismuth (209), lead (207), and mercury (200). A more commonly used measurement is density, which is expressed in specific gravity. The specific gravity of gold is 19.3, meaning it is 19.3 times heavier than an equal volume of water. Gold has two times the specific gravity of silver and nine times that of common quartz.

Anyone who has worked with gold knows how soft the metal is. On the Mohs mineral hardness scale—which rates talc, the softest mineral, at 1.0, and diamond, the hardest mineral, at 10.0—gold is rated at 2.5, harder than lead, but softer than copper. Nevertheless, gold melts at a surprisingly high temperature, 1063 degrees C., much higher than lead and about the same as copper.

Alchemists considered gold a "noble" metal, because of its resistance to fire, atmosphere and most solvents; that inertness, or chemical inactivity, is why gold occurs primarily as a free metal in nature. Although gold is usually found in its free metallic state, it always occurs in combination with other metals, usually silver, copper, iron and the platinum group metals. The secondary metal or metals present cause the color to vary considerably. Nearly pure gold has a characteristic rich, yellow luster; copper creates a warmer reddish hue, while silver and platinum may lighten the color to a near silver-white.

The most malleable and ductile of all metals, gold has an amazing capability to be flattened and molded. Not even extreme hammering irreversibly damages the metal; instead, the gold can be pounded into a delicate, film-like metallic leaf as thin as 1/300,000th of an inch. Gold coins stacked high enough for a long enough time will fuse together under their own weight. Its extraordinary ductility allows a single ounce of gold to be drawn into a continuous hair-like thread about sixty miles long.

Gold's remarkable properties—authoritative weight, workability, durability, and beautiful and distinctive color and luster, along with relative rarity—attracted the attention of early man. Bits of gold have been found in Spanish caves inhabited during the Paleolithic period, 40,000 years ago. Crudely hammered gold amulets dating back 12,000 years have been recovered from Stone Age caves in eastern Europe. Although gold was far too soft to be fashioned into tools and weapons, Neolithic peoples bestowed upon the metal a value far greater than its ornamental uses warranted. That intrinsic value stemmed from their veneration of the metal's unique properties. Gold became valuable simply because it was just that—gold.

By 4000 B.C. the early Egyptians had learned to melt gold, as well as to recover it from placer deposits by systematic gravitational separation—washing sand and gravel through troughs lined with sheepskins to trap and hold even the tiniest particles. The Greek legend of Argonauts and the Golden Fleece may have originated from an expeditionary raid about 1200 B.C. on a distant Egyptian placer mine where fine gold was recovered on sheepskins. By then, without the benefit of explosives or even iron tools, the Egyptians had begun lode-gold mining. They advanced their extensive underground workings by heating solid rock with open fires, then dashing it with cold water. Slaves exploited the cracks with stone hammers and wedges to break the rock, then hauled it to the surface.

Egyptian contributions to the technology of gold production went beyond mining to smelting and refining. Egyptian metallurgists constructed well drafted charcoal furnaces to melt small bits of gold from lode ores, then refined the metal by simple evaporation and condensation of gold vapors, achieving high levels of purity.

Gold became a monetary metal as early as 1000 B.C., when the Chinese began circulating small cubes of precise weights which quickly gained favor among merchants. Other standard weights that facilitated gold's growing monetary functions followed. Among the earliest was the *grain*, a weight unit equal to an average kernel of the local grain of the numerous cultures that used this measurement. More practical for trade was the Babylonian *shekel*, composed of 250 grains and roughly equal to a half ounce. By 700 B.C., the Greeks were issuing gold coins in standard denominations based upon weight.

*Early gold scale weights were usually calibrated in pennyweights. Twenty pennyweights (abbreviated "DWT") equalled one troy ounce.* —National Mining Hall of Fame and Museum

Our modern system of gold weights emerged during the Middle Ages with the Italian *florin* (48 grains) and the English tower pound (5,400 grains). The tower pound remained the English standard until a new system was introduced in the 1500s at the international trade fairs held at Troyes, France. Since then, the troy system has been accepted as the international weight standard for all precious metals, including gold, silver and the platinum group metals. The troy pound has twelve troy ounces; each troy ounce contains 20 pennyweight, with 24 grains to a pennyweight. Troy ounces are within ten percent of the avoirdupois—the sixteen ounce pound system we use in the United States—counterpart; one troy ounce contains 31.1 grams, while the avoirdupois ounce contains 28.35 grams. Today, international gold mining production figures are stated in metric tons, or tonnes, with each metric ton containing one million grams, or 32,154 troy ounces. The avoirdupois standard ton of 2,000 pounds is equivalent to 29,170 troy ounces and, interestingly, occupies only about one cubic foot. At a price of $400 per troy ounce, that one cubic foot of gold is worth nearly $12 million.

Because of the great softness of pure gold, early metallurgists developed alloys, usually with silver or copper, to enhance the hardness of the metal. The purity measurement system began with the *carat*, a weight based on the carob seed and originally used to weigh gemstones. Metallurgists adapted the carat for alloy purity measurement, making it the basic unit in a 24-unit scale. The letter "k" distinguishes it from gemstone weights; carat became karat. Twenty-four karat gold, then, refers to the pure metal; 18k refers to a 75 percent gold alloy, and 12k to an alloy containing only half gold. The karat system serves for jewelry and ornamental alloy measurement, but a 1,000-part fineness scale was devised for more precise metallurgical purposes. Pure, or 24k gold is 995 or 999 fine; 18k gold is 750 fine.

The word gold is thought to have originated with Sanskrit *jvalita*, from *jval*, meaning "to shine," and is derived directly from the Teutonic *gulth*, or "shining metal." The Spanish *oro* evolved from the Latin word for gold, *aurum*, or "shining dawn." *Aurum* still survives in the names of gold's two types of chemical salts, auric and aurous.

During the Middle Ages, a serious shortage of gold adversely affected trade and inspired many imaginative attempts to create the metal, most often from lead, silver or mercury. Although failing to create gold by transformation, the alchemists greatly improved amalgamation methods. Amalgamation, the ability of mercury to absorb half its weight in gold or silver, had been known since Roman times. Before the alchemists refined the practice, the amalgam was simply heated to drive off the mercury, leaving behind gold and silver of high purity. The alchemists constructed copper retorts to recover the mercury by condensation for reuse, and even devised accurate amalgamation assay techniques, effectively determining the gold content of a variety of ores. When Europe began its exploration of the New World, amalgamation was the universal method of efficiently recovering fine particles of gold from both placer gravels and crushed lode ores.

In the 15th century only about 300,000 troy ounces of gold—perhaps ten standard tons—existed in all of Europe. Unknown to the Europeans, an infinitely greater amount of gold had already been mined in yet unexplored South America, where early Incas had, since 800 B.C., been mining what were probably the richest placer deposits on earth. By 1400 A.D., when the Incan civilization reached its zenith, placer mining was a highly organized industry that may have produced ten tons of gold each year—by far the highest gold production of any culture at that point in history.

The Incan perception of gold was distinctly unlike that of the Europeans. Incas venerated gold. They never degraded it by using it as money, or as a symbol or store or personal wealth. They used it only in sacrifice and the most sacred religious art. They created magnificent gold work by hammering, annealing, gilding, fusing, casting and the use of almost every technique employed by modern goldsmiths with the exception of electroplating. The Inca's highly developed gold-working skills eventually spread as far north as the Aztec empire in Mexico.

Many historians consider Western civilization's greatest adventure to have been the exploration and exploitation of the New World, and cite three factors that motivated the Spanish to conquer most of a hemisphere: the gospel, glory and gold. The biggest factor may have been gold, for King Ferdinand's famed edict of 1511 defined the ultimate goal of the explorations: "Get gold, humanely if you can, but at all hazards, get gold."

The Spanish did indeed get gold, but rarely humanely. Hernán Cortés looted the Aztec empire in 1521, and within four years shipped over eight tons of gold to Spain. That conquest was overshadowed in 1533, when Francisco Pizarro overthrew the Incan empire, then used hostages and torture to accumulate the greatest golden ransom in history. Some four million ounces—140 tons—of Incan gold took six years to reach Spain, and represented the greatest infusion of gold into any economy up to that point in history. Almost all of the Incan gold was in the form of exquisite artwork, which the Spanish unceremoniously melted down into bars and coins.

The huge amount of gold seemed to confirm Spanish ideas of "El Dorado," a golden civilization, and even of a "golden man." Only after a century of searching failed to find "golden cities" did the Spanish begin systematic mining. For prospecting and small-scale washing, the Spanish used the wooden, conically shaped *batea*, which functioned exactly as our modern metal gold pan. *Bateas*, as large as four feet across, in the hands of two men could quickly wash fifty pounds of gravel.

Lode mining began in the late 1600s. Using hammers, crude iron drills, black gunpowder and slave labor, the Spanish worked rich quartz outcrops, crushing the ore in *arrastres* and recovering the gold by washing and amalgamation. The Spanish Crown closely controlled and heavily taxed this colonial mining industry.

Portugal made the next major gold strike in 1682 at Minas Gerais, deep in the interior jungles of Brazil. Minas Gerais was the first gold rush dictated by free enterprise. Portugal had no hope of establishing order or collecting its crown tax in the remote jungles, and individual adventurers, ranging from already wealthy noblemen to escaped slaves, competed for fortunes on fairly equal terms. The Minas Gerais residents used raw gold as currency, and many of the social and economic patterns they established in the Brazilian jungles were repeated in the coming gold rushes of the western United States.

Together, Spain and Portugal mined or looted an estimated 2,000 tons of gold from Central and South America over three centuries. Ultimately, both nations faced disastrous results; neither built industries to generate income internally, but used the gold to pay for wars, imports and more adventuring. By 1820 the Spanish and Portuguese colonial empires had collapsed before the rising forces of militaristic nationalism, and gold mining activity shifted to North America.

When the United States won its independence, the new government had three bases to chose from for a national monetary standard: gold, silver, or both. Alexander Hamilton favored gold, because, historically, its value had fluctuated the least. But the popular Spanish silver "dollar," the descendant of the internationally accepted "piece of eight," had given the American public far greater confidence in and familiarity with silver. Accordingly, Congress approved a compromise bimetallic monetary standard in 1783, with the silver-gold ratio set at 15:1. The federal treasury issued and maintained coinage at that approximate ratio, controlling the prices and markets of both metals.

Immediately following independence, the United States lacked significant mine sources of gold or silver. Traces of gold had been found in the Appalachians in the 1600s, but the first small placers weren't worked in North Carolina until 1792. A seventeen-pound nugget was found by a boy in a North Carolina creek in 1799. It served as a doorstop for several years until it was correctly identified as gold, touching off the first gold rush in the United States. Increasing placer production soon led to construction of a small United States Mint at Charlotte.

Richer placers were discovered in Georgia in 1829, luring 4,000 gold seekers onto land ceded in perpetuity to the Cherokee Nation. Partially because of its inability to stop the rush, the government rescinded the treaty and opened the land to gold mining after the fact. Georgia gold production peaked by 1837, and accounted for enough gold to warrant the government establishing another United States Mint at Dahlonega. By the 1840s the Appalachian goldfields had yielded an estimated 260,000 troy ounces of gold worth nearly $5

*A portable gold scale used in Central City shortly after the Pike's Peak gold rush.* —National Mining Hall of Fame and Museum

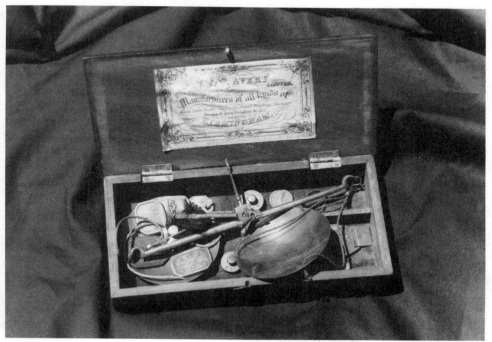

million, a welcome contribution to the struggling U.S. economy. The Appalachian goldfields also provided the United States with a tremendous learning experience. Americans became familiar with gold and how to mine it with the basic placer tools of rockers, sluice boxes and metal gold pans.

The greatest revelation these goldfields gave the country was certainly the utter simplicity of recovering gold from placer gravels by hydraulic gravitational separation, or "washing." The specific gravity of placer gold, because of the other metals present, can range from 15.0 to 19.0. Placer gold with a specific gravity of 18.0 is about seven times more dense than common quartz sands. In water, however, that difference becomes about ten times more pronounced (18.0-1.0/2.65-1.0, with 1.0 being the specific gravity of water). If you mix a panful of gravel thoroughly with water, then agitate it to keep it in a fluid state, any gold present almost immediately settles to the bottom, allowing the gravels at the top to be washed off. Repetitive washing quickly produces a concentrate of gold and other relatively heavy minerals, most of which will be the familiar "black sands"— iron-based minerals with specific gravities ranging from 4.3 to 5.2. Continued careful washing reduces the concentrate further, allowing you to easily recovery the coarse bits and flakes of gold. The finer particles are most efficiently recovered by amalgamation. Using the proper technique, it is nearly impossible to lose gold from a pan, except for the exceedingly fine "flour" or thin "leaf" forms lost through capillary action and electrostatic particle attraction.

The Georgia gold fields gave American metallurgists, chemists and even druggists the opportunity to become familiar with procedures to chemically identify gold. Aqua regia, a mixture of nitric and hydrochloric acids, was important to these assayers as one of the few known gold solvents. They could detect the presence of even trace amounts of gold, once dissolved, by the "purple of Cassius" test. Zinc dust and solutions of potassium cyanide and lead acetate were first added to precipitate out any gold present. The assayer then redissolved that precipitate in aqua regia. If gold was present, adding a few drops of a tin chloride solution produced a distinctive yellow to purple tint.

After the Appalachian gold experience, American assayers also became familiar with the ancient fire-assay process. In this quantitative process, the assayer first combined one accurately weighed part of a finely crushed sample with three parts of a mixture of lead oxide, carbonate of soda and silica, then fused the mix at about 1000°C. The high temperature reduced the lead oxide to molten lead, which dissolved any gold or silver present. The assayer then removed the slag and flux materials, leaving a button of lead-gold-silver.

When the assayer remelted the button in a cupel made of bone ash or magnesia, the cupel absorbed the lead, leaving only the gold-silver. Next, the assayer used nitric acid to dissolve and remove silver (and any other base metals present), leaving only pure gold. The weight of that gold, compared with the weight of the original sample, provided a grade of richness that has been traditionally expressed in troy ounces per standard ton.

In 1837 the Department of the Treasury adjusted its original 15:1 bimetallic monetary ratio to 16:1. The department also formally valued gold at $20.67 per troy ounce: to maintain the 16:1 ratio, it fixed the price of silver at $1.29 per troy ounce. Under the policy of "free coinage," both metals could be freely exchanged at all banks and U.S. Mints. The Treasury Department chose this basic ratio because it approximated the historic mine production ratios recorded over the previous two centuries. But, as America turned westward, events made it increasingly difficult for the government to maintain the nation's official bimetallic monetary standard.

The greatest internal mass migration in the nation's history began when gold was discovered in California in January 1848. In the East, Georgia in particular felt its effects; Georgians knew more about gold mining than did the residents in any other part of the nation. Many men, including John Beck, Louis Ralston, William Green Russell and John Gregory, joined the rush. In the West, the arrival of a quarter-million people and booming gold production made California a State of the Union in 1851.

In 1849—the first full year of mining—California produced 300,000 ounces of gold; that was more than the Appalachian mines yielded in fifty years. In 1851, production topped 2.6 million ounces worth about $50 million, considerably more than the entire annual expenditure of the federal government. And by 1857, with production in decline, California's cumulative yield was well over 20 million ounces—685 tons—worth about $400 million.

California gold meant instant international financial credibility for the United States, which displaced Russia as the world's leading gold producer. Much of California's gold went to England and France, which for decades had refused unsound U.S. dollars as payment for old debts. Gold coinage in Europe and the United States increased tenfold in just five years, with the gold in virtually every gleaming new coin originating in a California sluice box.

California gold had profound emotional and cultural effects on the American people, instilling in them a renewed faith in both their personal futures and the Nation's future. California proved that the West was real and, gold or not, offered a viable alternative to life in

41

the dreary East. The '49ers who joined the great trek became an indelible part of American folklore, with their adventures celebrated in both song—"I'm off to Californy with a washbowl on my knee"— and in the spoken word. Colorful and enduring expressions like "stake a claim," "see how it pans out," and "strike it rich" all originated in the excitement and adventure of the California gold rush.

But the gold rush in California had its greatest impact on the common person. Regardless of education, background, age or personal wealth, individuals could participate as equals in a major gold-seeking adventure with the chance to make a fortune, and to make it legally. They needed neither license, nor permission, nor titles before their names. They needed only to arrive early enough to stake a claim in their own names under the grassroots democracy of *de facto* mining district law. They kept every grain of gold they washed from their claims, paid no percentage to a distant king, nor any taxes even to their own government. Rather than special skills and investment capital, their greatest needs were common sense and the willingness to work and learn from others. For those who could arrive at the next strike fast enough, or even make that strike themselves, gold mining represented the epitome of free enterprise.

By 1858 many Americans were ready for another gold rush. Many in the East had missed the "first California," and many in California waited impatiently for the next one. They all got their chance when William Green Russell found gold along the South Platte River near the foot of the shining mountains.

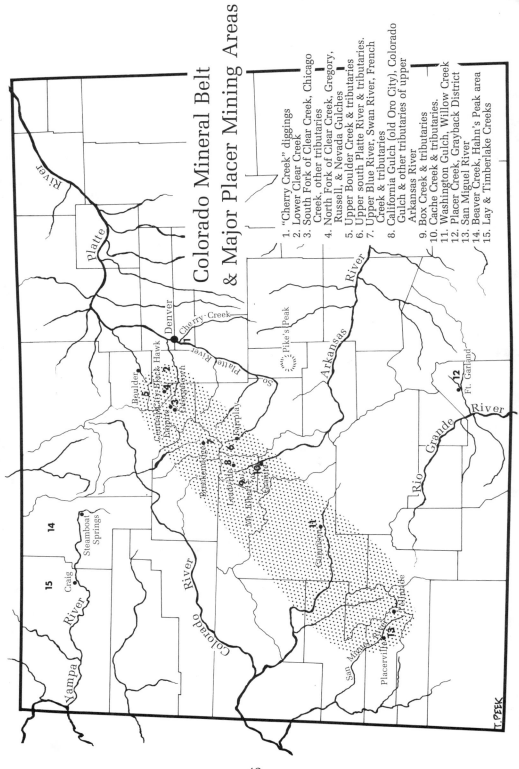

Colorado Mineral Belt & Major Placer Mining Areas

1. "Cherry Creek" diggings
2. Lower Clear Creek
3. South Fork of Clear Creek, Chicago Creek, other tributaries
4. North Fork of Clear Creek, Gregory, Russell, & Nevada Gulches
5. Upper Boulder Creek & tributaries
6. Upper south Platte River & tributaries.
7. Upper Blue River, Swan River, French Creek & tributaries
8. California Gulch (old Oro City), Colorado Gulch & other tributaries of upper Arkansas River
9. Box Creek & tributaries
10. Cache Creek & tributaries.
11. Washington Gulch, Willow Creek
12. Placer Creek, Grayback District
13. San Miguel River
14. Beaver Creek, Hahn's Peak area
15. Lay & Timberlake Creeks

43

*On Saturday last, Tom Groves and Harry Lytton . . . struck a pocket of gold nuggets from which they in four hours removed two hundred and forty-three ounces and nine pennyweights of gold. The largest nugget weighed fully one hundred and sixty ounces.*

—*Breckenridge Daily Journal*, July 25, 1887

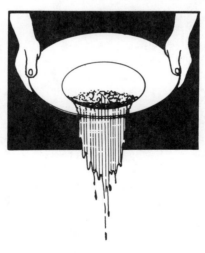

# 3

# THE SHADOW OF SILVER
## 1868 - 1893

By the late 1860s the excitement, along with the bonanza placers and the rich, oxidized outcrops of the Pike's Peak rush, was history. The future of gold mining in Colorado hinged on finding suitable methods to treat the refractory ores. The miners' first hope had been simple roasting, or "calcining," which oxidizes the sulfide minerals, driving off the sulfur and leaving behind gold and metal oxides that do not interfere with amalgamation. Roasting produces a fluffy, highly porous calcine of disintegrated rock, physically freeing more gold than is possible through stamp mill crushing. While technically simple, roasting is a time-consuming, expensive extra step practical only with higher grade ores. Amalgamation, of course, recovers only the gold and silver—it left in place the considerable quantities of lead, zinc and copper present in refractory ores of the Central City-Idaho Springs area.

In 1864 James E. Lyon shipped some selected high-grade sulfide ores to furnaces in New York, and learned that the lead component of ore might be the key to more efficient recovery of the gold and silver. Within a year, Lyon had several small furnaces operating in Black Hawk, two miles below Central City. In a fire assay, or cupellation process, Lyon recovered gold and silver using molten lead as the vehicle; the molten lead carried the gold and silver within it. Lyon then oxidized the lead melt in a blast of air; the lead oxide was absorbed into the bone ash cupels, leaving behind large buttons of gold-silver.

Nathaniel P. Hill, a New England chemist, advanced the smelting process when he established the Boston & Colorado Smelting Company at Black Hawk in 1867. Hill's small furnaces efficiently recovered gold and silver within a copper "matte", a mixture of metals and several simple compounds they form. Within a year the Black Hawk operation had poured 200 tons of copper-silver-gold matte; it contained only one percent gold, yet those 60,000 troy ounces represented two-thirds of the gold mined in Colorado Territory that year.

Unfortunately the heavy bars of matte had to be hauled by wagon to the Missouri River, shipped by rail to New York, and finally shipped on to Swansea, Wales, for refinement. The young smelting industry received some help when the railroad reached Denver in 1870. By the time the first refinery was constructed in Denver in 1875, about a dozen small smelters were operating in Colorado mining districts. All used only direct-smelting ores—ores rich enough to go straight into the furnaces—for metallurgists had yet to develop a practical method to concentrate lower grade ores.

The chlorination process of treating primary gold ores appeared in the early 1870s. The processors mixed chemical reagents with crushed gold ores, then heated the mixture in furnaces to liberate chlorine gas, a powerful oxidizing agent that quickly converted the metal to a soluble gold chloride. They then either vaporized the chloride in retorts and collected it as a solid condensate, or leached and collected it as a solution. The addition of zinc powder then precipitated the gold out of solution. Chlorination was over 90 percent efficient and immediately began replacing amalgamation in many primary gold mines. However, it was far from the ideal method of gold extraction. Reagents were costly, the process clumsy, and chlorine gas highly poisonous. Furthermore, chlorination worked poorly on complex ores containing base metals.

Among the biggest problems facing Colorado's infant lode-mining industry was underground mining itself, for miners had barely advanced over those of colonial times. Typical of Colorado's first generation of underground, or hardrock, mines were those at the head of California Gulch, near the largely deserted placer camp of Oro City. Horizontal tunnels or vertical shafts led to internal workings—horizontal drifts and vertical winzes—through which miners attempted to follow the often erratic veins of gold-laden quartz.

Drifts were rarely wider than a man's outstretched arms. Smaller workings meant better inherent ground support requiring less timber. But more important to miners was the sheer effort and expense

*In early Colorado gold mines, blast holes were drilled manually with the hammer and steel.*
—National Mining Hall of Fame and Museum

of breaking rock; they still manually drilled blast holes. In "single-jacking," a miner held a chisel-like steel in one hand and swung a four-pound sledge in the other. "Double-jacking" was faster; one miner gripped the steel with both hands, while one or two of his partners pounded away rhythmically with eight-pound sledges. In the brief moment between hammer blows, the miners had to "shake," or rotate, the steel a fraction of a turn to reposition the single cutting edge within the deepening hole—while remaining confident of the accuracy of the falling hammers. Drilling a single two-foot-deep hole could take an hour, depending upon the hardness of the rock and the enthusiasm of the drillers. Since the face of even a small drift required at least eight holes, hand drilling took most of the miners' effort and time, and the mine owners' expense.

When it came time to pack the drilled holes with explosives, the miners left the center hole of the patterns empty; they loaded all the others with black blasting powder in paper cartridges, tamped them gently with a wooden rod, and packed the ends with mud. The length of the protruding fuse determined the timing of each explosion. Inner holes detonated first, collapsing the rock into the empty center hole to create the hollow center "burn." Then the outer charges exploded, directing their energy inward toward the burn, thus breaking the rock in a planned configuration. Before lighting all fuses simultaneously, the miners laid a flat iron sheet on the floor before the face as a shoveling surface. The blast advanced the drift about two feet, and about four tons of broken rock, or "muck," awaited the shovels. Miners loaded the muck, either waste rock or ore, into small cars and hand-trammed it over light rail to the portal or to a shaft station, where they loaded it into buckets and raised it to the surface with a windlass.

Conditions for miners in the early hardrock mines were, at the very least, difficult. Dim, flickering candles or smoking oil lamps provided little light, and poor ventilation left the air clouded with rock dust, smoke and noxious gasses generated by blasting. By 1869 Oro City had four small hardrock mines, the American Flag, Five-Twenty, Pilot Tunnel and, the biggest producer, the Printer Boy. All were shallow mines that exploited only the oxidized portion of the veins; anything deeper meant refractory sulfide ores as well as the beginning of the water table and another expense—pumping.

Ore containing less than four or five ounces per ton rarely meant a profit for the mine owners, and miners never knew from one shift to the next how much they would find. The erratic, narrow veins could suddenly widen—"blossom"—into rich pockets, or just as quickly disappear—"pinch out"—into nothing. And the only way to learn what lay in the rock ahead was to tunnel into it.

Some of the first specimens of Colorado lode gold to be spared from the stamp mills came from the Printer Boy. The mine owners saved the delicate crystallized gold on white quartz not for its rarity, beauty or mineralogical value, but to display in the East, to lure investment capital from would-be investors.

When the Pike's Peak rush took place, most of what became Colorado was public domain, land owned by the federal government but otherwise unadministered and unassigned. The government based its mineral-claiming system on old Spanish and Mexican practices that had been modified in California, then adapted to specific conditions in Colorado by individual mining districts. The federal government first clarified its mining law in 1866, then formalized it with the General Mining Law of May 10, 1872. The "1872 Mining Law," as it is familiarly known, standardized and defined the claiming procedure from start to finish. It specified the size of both placer and lode claims and spelled out the requirements for discovery: location, or "staking;" recording, or filing legal notification with appropriate agencies; improvement, or performance of actual mining-related work; and patenting, or applying for full title to the land. Congress intended the 1872 Mining Law to encourage mineral exploration and development of the Western federal lands; in that sense, it was among the most successful and effective federal laws ever enacted. In Colorado, the prospectors quickly put the 1872 Mining Law to heavy use in claiming a series of bonanza lode discoveries, as they moved steadily southwest into the San Juan Mountains.

In 1860 Charles Baker and a small group of California Gulch prospectors visited the San Juans, finding traces of placer gold at Eureka, near the present site of Silverton. Over three hundred men, lured by exaggerated reports, rushed into the San Juans the following year to establish the camp of Animas City, near Baker's Bridge in La Plata County. They found little gold and a great deal of trouble from the Ute Indians, who resented the miners invading their lands. The prospectors gladly departed late in 1861, leaving the Utes in peace for one more decade.

The 1870 discovery of placer gold on Wightman Fork, high on South Mountain at the future site of Summitville, redirected miners' attention to the San Juans. A year later, the Little Giant vein was discovered in Arrastre Gulch, near Silverton. The Little Giant was the region's first paying lode. The miners pulled out and crushed only twenty seven tons of ore, but the rich grade—seven ounces of gold per ton—attracted a growing number of prospectors. The claims the prospectors staked were all illegal, since the San Juans had been ceded by treaty to the Utes. In 1872 the government ordered all miners out of the San Juans. When most refused to leave, Washington announced it would evict them, if necessary with federal troops. In the following uproar the administration realized it was political folly to place Indian rights above the quest for gold. Backing down, Washington ordered Felix Brunot, a U. S. Commissioner of Indian Affairs, to negotiate a settlement with the Utes. With the subsequent Brunot Treaty, signed on September 13, 1873, the Utes relinquished claim to 4 million acres—6,250 square miles—of mineral land in return for an annual federal payment of $25,000.

Prospectors surged into the San Juans, making a remarkable string of discoveries of large mineralized veins containing silver, base metals and gold, in both telluride and free metal forms. All of Colorado's gold deposits had been found at high elevations: Central City and Idaho Springs were both above 7,500 feet, and those at Breckenridge, Fairplay and Oro City were about 10,000 feet. But in the San Juans, most were found at or above timberline—11,300 feet or higher—where steep grades, heavy snow, avalanches and long, bitter winters complicated both prospecting and mining.

By 1873 rich, oxidized gold-bearing quartz veins had been discovered at 11,500 feet on South Mountain above Wightman Fork, reminiscent of those found in Gregory Gulch in 1859. The town of Summitville was founded, and stamp mills and amalgamation mills were built, turning out the first substantial amounts of gold from the San Juans.

In August of the same year two prospectors, George Howard and R. J. McNutt, explored the high peaks about eight miles northeast of Silverton. Allan G. Bird, in his book *Silverton Gold*, described their strike, as well as the rigors and dangers of high-mountain prospecting:

The jagged peaks jutted to heights of 13,450 feet above sea level. They camped for the night in the timber on the north side of Hurricane Peak. The following morning, after a light breakfast, in the early morning chill of late August, they climbed along the rocky ridges near the crest of Hurricane Peak. A few small quartz stringers were examined. Shortly before noon the snow-white billowing clouds, which seemed to form from nowhere, congregated into the black mass of threatening turbulence. Sharp flashes of lightning followed by ear-splitting claps of thunder preceded the cold deluge that caught Howard and McNutt in an area of barren rock well above the timberline. Both men huddled under what small projecting rocks they could find. Lightning at elevations over 13,000 feet is a frightening thing. The flashes of electricity travel horizontally between opposite sides of the valley with the roar of a freight train. The air becomes so charged with static electricity that one's hair will stand on end. The only protection is to lie flat, wait and hope. Storms of this type are a daily occurrence in late August. Both men were wet and cold. When the wind had blown the clouds into the next valley, McNutt suggested climbing to the top of the ridge to work the south-facing slope where the sun's rays would warm their chilled bodies. . . .

Just to the north of the lake was a huge white quartz vein cropping out, tinted by the telltale rusty color that often signifies gold. Sheer excitement gripped both men as they looked on the panorama below. The vein protruded a full 40 feet above the surrounding valley and was at least 60 feet wide. The descent to the lake was agonizingly slow. Each step had to be taken with utmost care to prevent the slide-rock from breaking loose, starting an avalanche which could squelch years of dreaming. The sun was now shining brightly as R. J. McNutt struck the rusty-colored rock enclosed between wide bands of white quartz and streaks of purple-black rock. A large chip of shining, silver-colored lead sulfide sparkled before his eyes. The vein could be traced for over 3,000 feet along the surface. McNutt placed his claim over the eastern portion of the vein and named it the Sunny Side.

Howard and McNutt had discovered one of Colorado's great mineral deposits, although, at the time, they could not begin to gauge its potential. They had even staked their claims illegally, for, like many prospectors in the San Juans, they jumped the gun on the Brunot Treaty. Fortunately for them, they refiled the claims legally the following year.

In 1874 gold, silver and base metals were discovered near Lake City; most notable was the Hotchkiss vein, which appeared to contain an unfamiliar form of telluride gold. In 1875 the Smuggler vein, 3,000 feet of it exposed, was discovered high above the camp of Telluride in what is now San Miguel County. The original discoverers failed to properly file their claims, which were "picked up" by others the following year. At the time, this switch in ownership of a misfiled claim was hardly a noteworthy event, for no one understood either the nature or the extent of the vein. Four years later, however, the vein was producing extremely rich ores for its new claimants.

In 1877 two Englishmen, William Weston and George Barber, found yet another large, mineralized quartz vein in 11,500-foot-high Imogene Basin, six miles southeast of Ouray. The vein contained almost one ounce of gold per ton, not quite rich enough to be worked profitably. Nevertheless, Weston and Barber staked claims, two of which they named the Gertrude and the Una.

With the exception of Summitville, none of the San Juan veins provided an immediate bonanza to their discoverers. No one understood the complex mineralization, and the high, rugged, remote San Juans had neither railroads nor smelters. Some of Colorado's greatest gold deposits had been discovered in the San Juans, but their time was to come later.

As Colorado gold mining shifted steadily toward lode deposits, placer mining also underwent change. The mining industry no longer concentrated on finding the next bonanza gulch, but on finding ways to efficiently mass-mine the lower-grade gravels they had left. The cost to wash a ton, or one cubic yard, of placer gravel by hand panning was about $20. For a miner to break even, therefore, that one cubic yard of dirt had to contain at least one ounce of gold. A rocker reduced the cost to $5; a big sluice box with a good supply of water reduced the cost of washing that cubic yard of gravel to only $1. But water itself had become a considerable expense as well as a business. By 1870 well over three hundred miles of water diversion ditches served Colorado's placer mines, one hundred miles of ditch in Summit County alone.

Little "shovel-in" mining still went on; instead most companies with consolidated claims employed ground sluicing, or "booming." These companies constructed dams with movable gates upstream; they built other dams some distance downstream to direct the water and sediments through large, reinforced sluice boxes as much as six feet wide. After filling the upstream dam, miners released the water in a "booming" torrent to erode away the entire channel. Repetitive booming eventually swept all the gold-bearing sediments through the big sluices and completely exposed the bedrock underneath, in some cases allowing visible pieces of gold to be picked by hand from crevices. Large scale ground sluicing reduced the cost of washing one cubic yard of gravel to about thirty cents.

Hydraulic mining was an even more efficient method of mass mining placer gravels. Proven in California, hydraulicking appeared in Colorado in the 1870s. A large supply of water, two or three hundred feet higher than the workings was necessary. Miners piped the water down from the storage areas, then directed it into heavy hoses and through nozzles, called "monitors", or "giants." Under thousands of pounds of pressure per square inch, the powerful water jets were capable of eroding away benches of gold-bearing gravel as high as fifty feet. To recover the gold, the jets of water swept enormous volumes of mud, silt and sand through big steel sluices. Hydraulic mining devastated river banks and polluted streams for miles; more important, in the placer miners' perspective, it reduced the cost of washing one cubic yard of gravel to less than ten cents.

Cache Creek, a tributary of the Arkansas River near the little town of Granite on the Lake-Chaffee County line serves as one of the best examples of the development of a Colorado placer-mining district. Discovered in 1859, Cache Creek would have been the premier placer deposit along the entire upper Arkansas River had it not been for the California Gulch bonanza near Oro City, seventeen miles to the north. Shovel-in mining on independent claims lasted but briefly. In 1862 the Cash [sic] Creek Ditch Company began work on a desperately needed ten-mile-long diversion ditch system. By 1865, most claims had been consolidated under the Gaff Mining Company of

*California Gulch, at Leadville, about 1875. Hydraulic mining methods are employed to erode away huge sections of banks to reach gold bearing gravels.* —National Mining Hall of Fame and Museum

Cincinnati, and were mined by ground sluicing. By then, the Cache Creek Park district had already yielded 11,000 ounces of gold worth about $200,000.

Ground sluicing lasted until 1883, when the Gaff Mining Company sold the property to a British group, the Twin Lakes Hydraulic Gold Mining Syndicate. The Twin Lakes syndicate immediately invested over $100,000 into expanding the water diversion ditch system, acquiring hydraulic mining equipment, and hiring the services of a 25-year-old British mining engineer named Ben Stanley Revett. Within a year, sixty men worked round-the-clock shifts on six five-inch "Little Giant" hydraulic monitors. Even with mining limited to five months because of the 9,000-foot elevation, the Twin Lakes Hydraulic Gold Mining Syndicate was one of few large placer mining operations in Colorado to pay its investors substantial regular dividends.

During the 1870s and 1880s Colorado's annual placer gold production had steadied at about 12,000 ounces per year, only a fraction of that of the glory years of the early 1860s. Any Colorado miner who needed further proof that placer mining was in serious decline found it when Chinese miners began arriving in the mid-1870s. At first claim owners welcomed them as cheap labor, but many local miners resented their buying or leasing claims on their own. By 1878 as many as five hundred Chinese miners were working on the Colorado placers, mainly in Gilpin, Clear Creek, Summit and Park counties. Chinese miners often paid claim owners $1 per day in a loose leasing arrangement to work admittedly poor gravels. Through hard work and smart mining, many were believed to have washed out from $3 to $5 in gold per day. Little of that gold ever went into Colorado's production records; these miners shipped virtually all of it directly to China as raw gold.

In the San Juans neither the topography nor the mineralogy had favored the formation of rich placer deposits. The one important exception, however, was the San Miguel River. Prospectors discovered placer gold near the headwaters at Telluride in 1875, and traced color seventy five miles downstream into Montrose County. The San Miguel River, over many years, produced some 9,000 ounces of gold, a respectable amount, but far less than the old bonanzas of Summit, Park and Lake counties. Nevertheless, the lower San Miguel River saw the development of one of Colorado's most ambitious and daring placer-mining projects. In 1885 prospectors found gold in the gravels of Mesa Creek, a San Miguel tributary nine miles below the present site of Uravan. The Montrose Placer Mining Company consolidated the claims and capitalized the operation with $5 million and placed

*Construction of the "Hanging Flume," about 1890, on the east wall of the Dolores River Canyon near the confluence with the San Miguel River.*
—Colorado Historical Society

the planning of a hydraulicking project in the hands of Col. N. P. Turner, an experienced California mining engineer. What followed illustrated the lengths to which Colorado placer miners went to obtain water. This description of Turner's water diversion project appeared in Frank Hall's *History of the State of Colorado*:

> . . . it was found necessary to tap the stream thirteen miles above, and carry the water by ditch and flume the entire distance. For more than six miles this flume is supported on brackets from an overhanging cliff, ranging from 100 to 150 feet above the river and from 250 to 500 feet below the summit of the gorge. In places the cliff hangs over at an angle of fifteen degrees and such water as escapes the flume strikes the opposite side of the river 100 yards from its base. A wagon road was constructed along the cliff at its apex, from which workmen were let down on ropes for the purpose of drilling into the face of the cliff, inserting

the iron brackets and setting the flume thereon. The flume is six feet wide and four feet high, and 1,800,000 feet of timber was consumed in its construction. Col. Turner was engaged for more than two years in perfecting this wonderful enterprise. It carries 80,000,000 gallons of water each twenty-four hours. Its grade is six feet ten inches to the mile, and its cost is something over $100,000. . . . Col. Turner's lowest estimate of the gold contents of the ground is 25 to 30 cents per cubic yard, and he washes down into the great main sluice from 4,000 to 5,000 yards daily. The gold is extremely fine, and can be saved only by the liberal use of quicksilver.

. . . In September, 1891, he had made no general "clean up" of the sluices, but had taken from the head about four or five balls of amalgam about the size of a hen's egg, as a partial indication of the precious metal being saved.

Unfortunately the "hanging flume," acclaimed as "one of the remarkable triumphs of engineering in Colorado," served little purpose. Mining ceased only eighteen months after Col. Turner completed the flume. The Montrose Placer Mining Company failed for the same reasons as most of the other operations along the San Miguel River failed—overpromotion and expensive construction projects based on inaccurate testing of the placer gravels.

Through the 1870s Colorado mining had shifted steadily toward silver. Rich silver ores were discovered first at Caribou and Montezuma, and by 1870 Georgetown was producing $1 million of silver per year. More silver was found at Mt. Lincoln in Park County, then at Lake City in 1874. Silver also appeared in most of the big mineralized veins found even higher in the San Juans.

One of the biggest silver strikes in the West was made in 1877, near old Oro City in California Gulch. California Gulch placer miners had long been troubled by a heavy gray sand that fouled their sluice box riffles. Metallurgists finally identified the sand as a rich lead-silver carbonate, and prospectors discovered huge silver deposits nearby. By 1880 old Oro City was swallowed by the city of Leadville, where hundreds of mines produced a combined $10 million in silver each year. Another major silver discovery followed at Aspen, and Colorado was suddenly a "silver state." Although gold gave Colorado its start, silver attracted both the railroads and the large amounts of capital necessary to build a booming milling and smelting industry. By the late 1880s Colorado's annual silver production had reached $30 million—seven times more than gold—and was still climbing.

Although overshadowed by silver, gold mining itself made a recovery in the 1880s, and nowhere was it more exciting then Farncomb Hill, at the head of French Gulch near Breckenridge. The

Breckenridge district had been a big gold producer, almost all of it from placers until 1878, when Harry Farncomb struck it rich on lode gold. Farncomb arrived in Breckenridge during the 1860 rush, settled in French Gulch and made a modest living placer mining. Like many other prospectors before him, Farncomb followed the trail of gold up French Gulch, seeking its lode source. No one had found prominent outcrops; nevertheless, Farncomb dug into the side of the hill and discovered a rich alluvial placer—an outcrop of gold-bearing quartz that had weathered in place. Farncomb found the gold not in rounded bits, but in twisted wires and delicate crystallized leaf shapes that showed no alluvial wear. Farncomb realized that the hill formed the source of much of the French Gulch placer gold, but the veins were so fragile as to be incapable of forming prominent outcrops.

Farncomb named his strike the Wire Patch and quietly went about mining. While he amassed a small fortune in alluvial gold, he also acquired much of the hill, not by conventional claiming, but by buying it an acre at a time. In 1880 Farncomb revealed his secret by depositing in a Denver bank several hundred ounces of the most spectacular-looking gold Colorado miners had ever seen. A horde of prospectors rushed up French Gulch to stake some of the action, only to learn the Harry Farncomb already owned everything in sight.

Bitter prospectors accused Farncomb of "cheating"—buying the land rather than staking and recording claims in the usual manner, which would have tipped them off to his discovery. A group of Denver mining promoters with interests in the Breckenridge area actually filed suit against Farncomb because he had acquired the land "in a devious manner." The following battle, known as the "Ten Years War," included the failure of a bank and a few businesses, a shoot-out in French Gulch that left three men dead and six more wounded, and lengthy legal maneuvering in which the attorneys struck it rich. Farncomb, meanwhile, discovered veins near his Wire Patch placer that became the Wire Patch Mine. The mine provided Farncomb with 7,000 ounces of gold worth about $140,000. He then sold out for a fortune, retiring as one of the wealthiest men in Colorado.

Vein discoveries on Farncomb Hill included the Ontario, Key West, Boss, Fountain and Gold Flake. Most of the gold occurred in brilliant, intricate wire, leaf and crystalline forms. Ore from the Ontario Mine earned a blue ribbon in the lode gold specimen display at the 1881 Colorado Industrial Exposition at Denver. Col. A. J. Ware controlled many of the Farncomb Hill properties, mining only the richest veins and leasing the remainder to independent miners. Miners paid a lease fee, assumed all operating costs and risks, and paid Ware a twenty five percent royalty, due in "free gold" the day after they mined it. The royalty permitted Ware to assemble the first big collection of Farncomb Hill gold.

Leasing was a gamble. Miners could lose everything if the veins pinched out. Then, too, if luck was with them and the veins blossomed into big pockets of picture rock, they could make a fortune, which is exactly what happened to two miners working a lease on the Gold Flake vein on July 23, 1887. Two days later, the Breckenridge *Daily Journal* reported their strike on the front page:

AN IMMENSE NUGGET OF GOLD

On Saturday last Tom Groves and Harry Lytton who are working a lease on the Fuller placer patent on Farncomb Hill struck a pocket of gold nuggets from which they in four hours removed two hundred and forty three ounces and nine penny weights of gold. The largest nugget when taken out weighed fully one hundred and sixty ounces, two pieces were broken off leaving the nugget now shown weighing 136 oz. 5 dwt. which is we believe the largest nugget ever found in the state. Yesterday hundreds of visitors called on Col. Ware at his office at the concentrator on the west side, to feast their eyes on the find.

. . . Although this vicinity during the 1st two years has sent out thousands of fine specimens of nugget gold this one dwarfs them all. It will be sent to Col. Carpenter [Ware's partner] in Denver that Denverites may learn that there are other induce-ments in Colorado besides Denver town lots.

"TOM'S BABY"

When the big nugget of gold was found on Saturday afternoon by Tom Groves and Harry Lytton, Tom was so elated and fondled the find so affectionately that the boys declared that it was "Tom's Baby" and so it goes. It will probably be a long time before "Tom's Baby" will be retired as Colorado's big nugget."

136 OZ. 5 DWTS.

That is Summit County's latest champion nugget. Where is the district that can knock that chip off our shoulders in 1887?

. . . even in its native bed it was surrounded by a greater amount of gold than was contained in itself. . . .

Technically, "Tom's Baby" was not a nugget, that is, it was not a piece of worn, alluvial gold mined from a placer. It was a large mass of lode gold that was part of the original underground vein before it was mined.

The Farncomb Hill gold occurred in three principal crystalline forms: leaf, wire, and sponge-like arborescent growths. Leaf gold was most common, usually appearing as clusters of flattened eight-sided crystals as much as six inches long. The wire gold specimens, for which the Wire Patch placer and mine were named, were rarely more than one inch long and about one millimeter in diameter. Some individual wires five millimeters (about one-quarter inch) in diameter were found, and wires sometimes grew in dense, tangled masses called "bird's nest" gold. The arborescent growths were up to three inches long, somewhat flattened, and so delicate as to have a "spongy" feel.

About 900 fine, the Farncomb Hill gold had a brilliant luster and rich yellow color. There seemed to be a limitless variety of forms; some individual pieces were named for fanciful shapes, such as the "dragon," the "sailboat," and the "jackrabbit." Farncomb Hill gold had another distinction apart from its per-ounce monetary value: It was the first Colorado gold ever collected for its beauty, rarity of form and mineralogical significance.

The gold of Farncomb Hill enriched collections all over the world, probably to a greater extent than official production figures indicate. Farncomb Hill was Colorado's first experience with rampant "high-grading", or mine theft; working miners stole from their lessee bosses, lessees stole from lessor mine owners, and, on at least one occasion, mine owner partners stole from each other. Noted Colorado geologist and educator Arthur Lakes, writing in 1911 in *The Mining World*, believed more Farncomb Hill gold "was probably sold as specimens and stolen by miners than was ever shipped by the owners."

The same year that "Tom"s Baby" made headlines, other remarkable gold specimens came out of the Ground Hog Mine, near Red Cliff in Eagle County. Unlike the other nearby gold and silver mines, the Ground Hog had almost no lead or zinc in its ores. Gold and silver occurred in two vertical veins, or "chimneys," ranging in thickness from only a few inches to six feet. In one chimney, the gold occurred as tiny individual crystalline grains cemented together by iron minerals and "horn" silver. But in the adjacent chimney, the gold was formed into spectacular, massive wires known as "ram's horns."

The biggest of the many ram's horns the Ground Hog produced weighed eight ounces, measured one inch in diameter at the base and five inches in length, and branched gracefully into five distinct curls. One of the mine's owners purchased it for its "curious shape." The bullion value of the specimens was about $150, but, as the newspapers reported, it probably "had an increased value due to its curious and rare formation." That casual appraisal eventually became one of the greatest understatements of valuation of gold specimens ever made; in the early 1980s insurance appraisers valued the ram's horn at $750,00, or $95,000 per ounce.

During the 1880s Summitville was Colorado's largest gold producer. The Little Annie vein had been a miner's dream—shallow, completely oxidized and containing as many as five to ten ounces of gold per ton. At an elevation of over 11,300 feet, Summitville was the highest town in North America and usually cut off from the outside world during the six long months of winter. By 1890 Summitville had produced well over 100,000 ounces of gold worth $2.2 million, but the rich ores were gone and the high-mountain camp fell into decline.

Other mines, however, picked up the slack in gold production. Gold was discovered at the Sunnyside in 1882, one of the many mines in the San Juans that benefited from the arrival of the railroad and the growth of a smelting industry. Up to five ounces of gold per ton added substantially to the profits coming from lead, silver and copper. By 1890 the Sunnyside mill was conducting some of Colorado's earliest experiments in concentrating ores.

In the 1880s, four years after its discoverers misfiled their claim and lost their right to exploit it, the new claimholders realized the size and richness of the Smuggler vein when ores containing up to 800 ounces of silver and 15 ounces of gold were discovered. In 1891 the Smuggler-Union Mining Company consolidated the original claims, the Smuggler, Union, Mendota and Sheridan. Production soon reached $1 million a year in gold alone, some of it in beautiful specimens. One 17-pound piece came into the possession of mine owner John A. Porter, who donated it to the Colorado Scientific Society. Cut in half and polished to display the visible gold, the piece earned medals at the 1893 World Columbian Exposition in Chicago, and again at the 1900 Paris Exposition.

At Lake City, the Hotchkiss vein, since its discovery in 1874, had produced lead-silver and small quantities of gold. After periods of inactivity, so much gold was discovered in 1889 that the vein was renamed the Golden Fleece. A single two-ton ore car filled with petzite, a silver-gold telluride, yielded $50,000, mostly in gold. Just as at Farncomb Hill, the Golden Fleece was hard hit by high-grading miners. Many thousands of dollars worth of nearly pure petzite was thought to have "gone home" in miners' pockets.

By 1892 Colorado's gold production had climbed to 270,000 ounces, worth $5.4 million, the highest ever. That total would still rise, however, thanks to yet another golden surprise coming from another "old" mine—Leadville's Little Jonny. The Little Jonny was developed in 1879 at the height of Leadville's silver boom. The mine had been a good producer of silver and lead, but by the early 1890s seemed to have run out of ore when it came under the control of John F. Campion. Campion, a native of Canada, had arrived in Leadville in 1879 to become a successful claim broker. By 1890 Campion and his associates were able to buy mining properties outright. One was the Little Jonny, which became part of Campion's Ibex Mining Company.

In 1893 Campion hired a new mine superintendent, James Joseph Brown, and invested $30,000 to find more ore in the Little Jonny. Brown managed to timber his way through some notoriously unstable sandy dolomite that had stopped earlier miners, finding large deposits of high grade gold-copper ore—some of it grading fifteen ounces to the ton—that paid back Campion's $30,000 hundreds of times over. By 1894 the Little Jonny was paying its investors $1 million per year, and exploration was proceeding feverishly on what was already named the "Leadville Gold Belt." James J. Brown took his place in history not as the maker of a million-dollar gold mine, but as the husband of Margaret Tobin Brown—the "Unsinkable Molly Brown," who gained international fame for her heroism during the sinking of the *Titanic* in 1912.

John Campion, through his Wapiti Mining Company, also bought into some rich properties on Farncomb Hill in Breckenridge. An avid collector of native gold specimens, Campion amassed one of the world's most spectacular private gold collections, most of it coming from the Little Jonny and the other Ibex properties and, especially, Farncomb Hill. Campion actually purchased choice gold specimens from his own miners, a policy some other mine owners criticized as absurd. Campion not only paid wages, but spent additional money to "buy gold that already belonged to him." While the policy prevented many fine specimens from going to the stamp mills, it probably also prevented far more from going home in miners' pockets. Campion's gold won a first place award at the 1893 World Columbian Exposition in Chicago, and Farncomb Hill gold went on to take a blue ribbon at the 1904 World's Fair in St. Louis.

The nation's bimetallic monetary standard and the relative values of gold and silver had increasingly concerned the government since the Civil War. By 1870 gold had become undervalued, and public confidence in silver began to wane. Congress passed the Coinage Act of 1873, omitting the free coinage of silver and effectively, but not yet officially, placing the nation on a gold monetary standard. Silver could still be spent as money, but no longer exchanged at banks and U.S. Mints for gold.

By 1886, because of mine oversupply and a weak international market, the price of silver fell below $1 per troy ounce. Although the one-troy-ounce silver dollar could still be spent at its face value, it no longer contained one dollar's worth of silver. Just what to do with the flood of silver pouring from the western mines became the burning political issue of the era. Although Treasury stockpiles far exceeded any foreseeable coinage demands, the government still bought huge amounts of silver, creating a market to support the price. The "silver question" soon evolved into a sectional debate. Most eastern interests favored official adoption of the gold standard and the abandonment of silver. But silver mining was vital to the welfare of the western economy, and "silver bloc" politicians fought for increased government silver purchases. The silver bloc won the first round when Congress passed the Sherman Silver Purchase Act of 1890, requiring the Treasury to purchase 54 million ounces of unneeded silver annually, keeping many western mines in operation by raising the price back to $1.05 per ounce.

The nation's enormous silver production, however, made the effort futile. By 1893 the price of silver had fallen to seventy-eight cents per troy ounce, and Congress repealed the Sherman Silver Purchase Act. Silver fell immediately to sixty-three cents and hundreds of marginal silver mines closed, throwing miners out of work. Although people, especially in the West, viewed the collapse of the silver market as a regional economic catastrophe, gold was waiting to take up the slack. Many of Colorado's out-of-work silver miners found ready employment in lode-gold mines, and many others returned to the old placers, where gold still waited in the well-worked gravels. On August 26, 1893, *The Engineering and Mining Journal* offered this assessment of Colorado's mining future:

> Not all the Colorado miners are ready to throw in the sponge, or to accept the statement that silver is the sole interest upon which their State depends as have been the few speakers who have assumed to be their mouthpiece. Colorado was a gold state before it was a silver one, and it was the gold placers that first drew attention to Pike's Peak and the neighboring mountains, and to-day, according to the statements of local authorities, not a few of those who have been temporarily thrown out of work by the stoppage of the silver mines and the smelters have returned to their first love and gone back to the placers. Old districts which were abandoned because they did not pay the exorbitant rates of living which prevailed years ago are being reopened and careful search is being made for new ones. That this has already had its effect is shown by the fact, noted by the *Denver Republican*, that the gold deposits at the Denver Mint in July exceeded

by $60,000 those of any previous month in its history. Part of this doubtless came from the working of gold mines, but it is altogether probable that some of it is the result of the recent increase in placer mining. . . .

It is not impossible that the State has a future before it in which silver will play so subordinate a part that men will look back to some of the utterances of the present day with simple wonder at their folly.

The editors of *The Engineering and Mining Journal* could not have known the portent of their last statement. For the next quarter-century, the nation again equated Colorado with gold instead of silver. And the first step toward this equation was made in a cow pasture high on the southwest shoulder of Pike's Peak called Cripple Creek.

*If these eastern people want gold, we'll give them
gold until they're sick of it.*

—Cassius C. Smith, Ass't. General Manager
Denver & Rio Grande Railroad
October 13, 1895

# 4

# CRIPPLE CREEK

Early in the Pike's Peak rush some ill-informed gold seekers bound for the "Pike's Peak country" took that general name for the western Kansas goldfields literally, heading not for Cherry Creek, but for Pike's Peak itself, the majestic, 14,110-foot mountain one hundred miles to the south. They found the mountain made almost exclusively of a coarse, pink granite disappointingly barren of gold. While a fine regional landmark, Pike's Peak hardly seemed a fitting name to associate with Colorado gold.

After the initial furor of the rush, every stream along Colorado's Front Range, including those on Pike's Peak, were carefully prospected for gold. Prospectors probably found traces of a fine, flour-like gold in a broad depression 9,500 feet high on the mountain's western shoulder. But it fell short of being dug from the rich placers of Summit, Park and Lake counties, and the prospectors moved on. Twenty years later, that broad depression was the site of Cripple Creek, a Spartan collection of ranches and homesteads strung along its namesake—a creek with a treacherous rocky bottom notorious for laming cattle.

Cripple Creek's adventure with gold began in a negative fashion in 1884, when some local entrepreneurs decided to boost property values by staging a strike. They salted a few holes with placer gold, then "discovered" them. Hundreds rushed to the lonely site, only to leave with the bitter memory of having participated in the "Mt.

Pisgah Hoax." Respected mining men laid the hoax to rest with the pronouncement that, if gold was indeed "where you found it," then Cripple Creek would be the last place on earth to look for it.

In truth, Cripple Creek sat squarely atop on of the greatest concentrations of high-grade gold in North America. It had, in fact, already been discovered, not by one of those respected mining men whose words most prospectors heeded, but by a drifter described as a "part-time cowboy and full-time drinker" named "Crazy Bob" Womack.

Womack left his native Kentucky and joined the last of the stragglers of the Pike's Peak rush, arriving in Colorado in 1861. He spent several years in Idaho Springs, learning about gold and prospecting but never finding anything worth his time. Eventually, he settled in Cripple Creek, earning a meager living as a ranch hand and still looking for gold in his spare time. He found some in 1879—a single piece of loose, alluvial "float," an unfamiliar, fine-grained volcanic rock that assayed out to a remarkable ten ounces of gold per ton. For ten long years, Womack tried unsuccessfully to find its lode source by digging hundreds of shallow, barren prospect holes, a stubborn endeavor that earned him the nickname "Crazy Bob."

Womack's perseverance finally paid off in 1890. Grubstaked by a Colorado Springs dentist, he sank a narrow shaft thirty feet with a pick and shovel—straight into a gold deposit that would soon be known as the El Paso lode. Womack filled a sack with samples that assayed out at eight to ten ounces per ton. But when he joyously announced his strike, he received almost no response. The names of Cripple Creek and Crazy Bob were without credibility. Womack was only able to sell a half interest in the El Paso lode for $500.

Although Womack's high-grade samples failed to attract investors, they did attract other prospectors, among them a broke Colorado Springs carpenter named Winfield Scott Stratton. Stratton made a strike on his own six miles south of Cripple Creek at the future site of Victor. Unlike Womack, Stratton didn't sell out cheap; instead, he bought out his partner for $500, becoming sole owner of the property that became the Portland Mine. In less than a year, Stratton and a handful of hired miners dug out $200,000 in gold ore, and the rush to Cripple Creek was on.

In 1893 the Cripple Creek district, now swarming with well over 10,000 miners, prospectors, speculators and promoters, produced $2 million in gold, about one-third of Colorado's entire output. That production was the beginning, for the hundreds of shafts that progressed deeper each day slowly revealed the enormity and richness of the deposit.

Cripple Creek's gold occurred within a small volcanic formation surrounded by gold-barren Pike's Peak granite. Geologists first thought the volcanic rock was a crater, then correctly determined that it was a caldera, or collapsed volcanic system. Some 35 million years ago the magma that formed the ancient Cripple Creek volcano withdrew, allowing the entire volcanic system to collapse inward. The broad depression that formed above the subsiding caldera filled with water and sediments, including volcanic and nonvolcanic rocks, which cemented together into a breccia. Continuing subsidence caused repetitive fracturing and recementing, eventually forming a complex breccia "neck" about 3,000 feet deep. Renewed volcanic surges then forced magma through the fractured breccia, creating pipes and dikes of volcanic rock. Between the surges of magma, hot mineral-bearing solutions were injected through the breccia, impregnating many of the rocks with gold, which sometimes crystallized into extraordinarily rich veins and pockets.

Some gold was present as a free metal, but most occurred as the telluride minerals calaverite and sylvanite. Tellurides appear physically similar to simple sulfides, such as galena (lead sulfide) and sphalerite (zinc sulfide); all are heavy, soft, brittle, and have a distinct metallic luster. Calaverite, a ditelluride of gold, has a lustrous brass-yellow to silver-white color similar to pyrite, and forms striated, elongated crystals. Sylvanite, a telluride of gold and silver, is heavy, extremely soft, and has a steel-gray color. The amount of silver in the two minerals varies; technically, when silver replaces 13.4 percent of the gold in calaverite, the mineral becomes sylvanite.

Roasting tellurides easily drives off the tellurium, leaving behind bubbles of gold or gold and silver. The "light roast" requires only enough heat to drive off the tellurium, leaving frothy metallic bubbles of gold suitable for further assay or refinement work. The higher heat of the "dead roast" produces solid beads of gold-silver that give an excellent visual indication of a sample's value.

The Cripple Creek deposit did not form the extensive placers that would have led to its discovery thirty years earlier for two reasons: the caldera had collapsed inward leaving no outcrops to erode away into alluvial gravels. And most of the gold occurred as tellurides; weathering and oxidation of tellurides produces gold so fine that it eludes all but the most careful panners.

The Cripple Creek deposit required deep mining, and, technologically, the timing was perfect. Mechanical drills appeared in Colorado in 1868, and by the time the Cripple Creek mines were operating the heavy, awkward and unreliable early models had been greatly improved. By 1890 the big pneumatic drills were "making hole" faster than the old hand drillers ever dreamed; only smaller mines still used hammers and hand steels, unable to afford the expense of the new drills, and the engines and compressors that went with them. "Giant powder"—powerful nitroglycerine dynamites that could "pull" holes six and even ten feet deep, dramatically speeded up the basic process of breaking rock—replacing the old black blasting powder.

When the Cripple Creek ores were discovered, gold extraction technology was limited to amalgamation, chlorination, and, for

*Drilling in the Independence Mine in the Cripple Creek District about 1895. These powerful, early pneumatic rock drills were called "widowmakers." Since they did not use water, they produced great clouds of dry silica dust which induced silicosis in many of the miners who used them.* —Colorado Historical Society

suitable ores, direct smelting using molten base-metal "vehicles" to carry off the gold. Mills first treated Cripple Creek ores by chlorination, but engineers and chemists were already studying a new process destined to profoundly change gold mining worldwide—cyanidation. The ability of cyanide to dissolve gold was discovered in Germany in 1846. A practical process to extract gold from ore with a weak, alkaline potassium cyanide solution was patented in Scotland in 1887, and the first cyanidation plant appeared in the New Zealand gold fields the following year. The process was patented in the United States in 1889, and eighteen months later a cyanidation mill was extracting gold from ores in Utah.

Although free-gold ores could be treated directly with cyanide solutions, refractory ores, including tellurides, required preparatory roasting. The mills mixed crushed ores with a dilute potassium cyanide solution to dissolve the gold and silver. They then collected the "pregnant' solution and treated it with powdered zinc to precipitate the gold-silver as a metallic sludge. The process was faster, simpler, less expensive, and, although the cyanide was highly poisonous, altogether less dangerous than chlorination. The biggest problem was the costly zinc precipitation step that limited cyanidation to a batch-type operation. Mills first used cyanidation on Cripple Creek ores in 1895; for the next decade, it competed closely with chlorination as the preferred gold extraction process.

The gold industry developed Cripple Creek swiftly and surely; investment capital poured in, mine owners consolidated claims into large properties exploited by large-scale, systematic mining supervised by top engineers, and printed and sold gold-mining stock certificates by the ream. In 1895 Colorado's gold production rocketed to 660,000 ounces worth about $13.2 million. Half of it came from booming Cripple Creek.

The timing of the collapse of the silver market and the Cripple Creek gold boom raised eyebrows, especially in the East, where "goldbugs" had petitioned long and hard for the repeal of the Sherman Silver Purchase Act. Some seriously believed that Colorado mining and railroad interests had somehow orchestrated the Cripple Creek boom as an act of spite. The comments of executives in these industries often reinforced such ideas. Cassius C. Smith, assistant general manager of the Denver & Rio Grande Railroad—one of the lines that profited handsomely from the strike—spoke at a promotional dinner in Colorado Springs, noting the sharply increasing production of gold at Cripple Creek, and bragging, "If these Eastern people want gold, we'll give them gold until they're sick of it."

Cripple Creek gold quickly made a number of millionaires, former carpenter Winfield Scott Stratton foremost among them. During 1895 Stratton's Portland Mine paid investors $120,000 every month. Not everyone, however, shared Colorado's boundless faith in Cripple Creek. *The New York Times* sent an investigative reporter to the camp for the firsthand look. The *Times*, which thirty-five years earlier had endorsed and promoted the tragic first phase of the Pike's Peak rush on nothing more than rumor, offered this cautious, even critical view of Cripple Creek on December 25, 1895:

### THE CRIPPLE CREEK FIELD

#### MARVELOUSLY RICH ORE, BUT IN SMALL VEINS
#### DIFFERS FROM OTHER MINING BOOMS

CRIPPLE CREEK, Dec. 24—Cripple Creek is undoubtedly a center of attention at the present time. For many years, not, indeed, since Leadville, has there been a mining camp in the Rockies so well advertised. It is the prime subject of discussion in Colorado from one end to the other; it is the chief theme of interest in every edition of the four daily papers of Denver; several journals of New York and Chicago have dispatched staff correspondents to the scene, which indicates an awakening of curiosity in the East; numerous mining exchanges for trading in Cripple Creek shares have been organized, and speculation is rife. In short, there is a veritable Cripple Creek "boom," but withall to the conservative observer, it appears largely artificial; it seems to lack the spontaneity that characterized the Leadville "boom," the Tombstone "boom," and others of the past. The fact is patent that while Cripple Creek is unmistakably a good mining camp, its resources are being enormously exaggerated.

. . . As to the permanence of the Cripple Creek deposits, but little can be vouchsafed, since there are few of the mines which have been systematically explored, or even opened beyond moderate depths. . . . Of the great majority of claims of the district, most are being operated under lease, and it is doubtful if they are profitable at all, and, if so, only in a small way.

Abundant evidence of this is Cripple Creek Town, which, notwithstanding the "boom" and the advertising that has been given it, impresses the visitor as a place in which little money is current. There are few of the accompaniments of mining excitement of former times. The scene is properly set. Rude cabins, saloons with sham fronts, dirty, uncomfortable hotels, rough streets, alternating deep with mud and dust, plank sidewalks following no special grade, with knots and nails unpleasantly prominent, the whole straggling amid the stumps of a devastated pine forest, with the brown, bare mountains towering in the distance. All of this is in accord with the preconceived notion

70

of a lively mining camp. The actors are also on stage. Men in rough corduroy clothes or canvas jackets stained with the grime of the mines, wearing broad-brimmed hats, and trousers tucked into boots; men in groups on the street corners or lounging in front of the hotel discussing the latest new "strike" or a pending sale; the stage and six swinging down the main street . . .

Most of these [Cripple Creek mining companies] are incorporated at the capital of 1,000,000 shares of $1 each, which are selling from one cent per share upward. The low-priced shares

*Underground gold miners at Cripple Creek pack onto "cages" for their descent at the beginning of their shifts, about 1900.*
—National Mining Hall of Fame and Museum

are great favorites with the women, who see in them an opportunity to speculate with a small amount of money and doubling and tripling it at the first turn. This craze affects all classes of people, to the ladies of Capitol Hill, Denver, to their cooks and servants. . . . No one takes the trouble to investigate the character of the stock they are buying. It is sufficient to know that it is cheap and the rest is left up to lucky chance.

   . . . The Portland, for instance, is paying its investors $60,000 per month in dividends [it was actually paying $120,000 per month] and is selling on the basis of $6,000,000 for its property. . . . In order to pay $60,000 in dividends, it will probably have to produce $12,000,000 in ore, and apart from the Comstock bonanzas there are very few mines, gold or silver, since the first discovery of gold in California, which have produced as much as that.

*The New York Times* was dead wrong in its assessment of Cripple Creek being just "another Rocky Mountain mining camp" that would fail to live up to its advertising. The Portland Mine alone produced not $12 million, but $60 million. In 1897 the diminutive, four by six mile Cripple Creek mining district produced a half-million troy ounces of gold worth $10 million. Incredibly, it only then hit its stride. Cripple Creek had its best year in 1900, when 475 mines turned out 900,000 troy ounces—about 30 standard tons—of gold worth $18.2 million, accounting for two-thirds of all the gold mined in the United States. Coinciding with Cripple Creek's record production, Congress fittingly passed the Gold Standard Act, formally placing the nation on a gold monetary standard. Nor was Cripple Creek destined only for brief glory. It remained the top gold district in the United States for fifteen consecutive years, and its annual production stayed above $10 million until 1918.

Cripple Creek ore was some of the richest ever found. Miners sometimes came off shift speaking in hushed tones of "veins that were damned near pure gold." To fully appreciate the richness of some of the best ores, keep in mind that one standard ton of pure gold contains just over 29,000 troy ounces and, at this era's prevailing price of $20.67, was worth about $600,000. One large mass of coarse wire gold from the Cardinal Mine was graded as "800 fine," for its value of $500,000 per ton. A single railcar load of ore from the Isabella Mine consigned to an extraction mill in Colorado Springs was valued at $219,000. The load only weighted 28 tons, but each ton weighed 390 ounces of gold worth $7,800. The Isabella also yielded one celebrated piece of metallic gold that was too large for the ore sacks. Miners tried to break it but the gold content was so great that the rock merely bent. Cripple Creek may have been the only gold district in the United States where shipments were sometimes graded in dollars per pound instead of the traditional troy ounces per ton. Selected ores from the Rubie Mine assayed at $65 per pound, equal to 6,500 ounces of gold worth $130,000 per ton. To the miners in the underground workings of the richest mines, it seemed gold was everywhere. During one week in 1903, three miners panned the drainage ditches of the Portland Mine, washing out 25 ounces worth nearly $500.

Across the nation, Cripple Creek became an ideal of production and profits, with resulting dividends measured in the millions of dollars. But another side to the Cripple Creek story was one of thousands of miners subjected to back-wearying labor in a dark, dreary and dangerous environment, miners suffering splitting headaches from the nitroglycerine fumes, debilitating lung diseases from inhalation of rock dust, and injury and even death from frequent mine accidents. Many miners distrusted mine owners and harbored bitter memories of the violence-marred Cripple Creek labor disputes and strikes that earned them nothing more than a three-dollar-wage for an eight-hour shift. The owners made millions, but it was the poor miner who first handled those fabulously rich ores. With a single piece of gold the size of a marble worth $20—more than an entire week's pay—it was understandable that many miners succumbed to the inevitable temptation.

High-grading, the theft of gold by miners, was a common practice in the goldfields of the American West and, for that matter, in any gold-mining region of the world. It began in the placers with hired laborers pocketing an occasional nugget or "riffle pinch." Simple supervision controlled high-grading in the placers, but the hardrock mines were different; miners had little supervision in the dark underground, and long shifts to devise clever ways to get around company security measures. Mine owners considered high-grading blatant theft, a crime no different than robbing a bank. Yet miners who also felt theft was wrong, and who wouldn't think of stealing a loaf of bread, considered high-grading an earned right, justifying it by weighing it against the physical risk, underpayment, terrible working conditions and even the "right of discovery," since they "discovered" the gold in the course of drilling and blasting.

Colorado mine owners had been troubled by high-grading since the crystalline gold of Farncomb Hill was discovered, and had been unable to halt the practice at mines like the Smuggler-Union, the Golden Fleece and the Little Jonny. But when Cripple Creek boomed, high-grading flourished as never before. As early as 1895 the troubles of Colorado gold mine owners rated a feature article in *The New York Times:*

COLORADO'S MINE THIEVES

PROBABLE THEY HAVE STOLEN ORE
WORTH MILLIONS OF DOLLARS

NO DOUBT THEY HAVE AN ORGANIZATION
AND CAREFUL METHOD OF ROBBING

MANY MINE OWNERS SUFFER

Denver, Colo., June 16.—Discovery of the thefts of rich ore from the Golden Fleece Mine has led to the belief that ore worth millions of dollars has been stolen from the mines of Colorado in the last ten years by an organized band. . . .

The loss sustained by the Fleece is now place at $70,000, or more than the actual dividends of the mine. The Fleece yesterday paid the June dividend, but ordered a suspension of all work on the mine until the responsibility for the stealing is placed. . . .

Among the other mines that are said to have suffered from the smugglers are . . . the Victor and Pike's Peak of Cripple Creek. Bonanza ore runs from $1,000 to $20,000 a ton, and the method of cheating the owners is simple. From rich blocks of ore corners are knocked off and carried away in the pocket. Small pieces of rich ore run from $10 to $30 in cubes of about two inches. . . .

The Victor Mine last week discovered that the richest ore was being stolen by some means that defied all attempts to trace. Returns on the surface did not agree with reports from the underground works, and investigation showed that lots of rich ore was not coming to the surface on account of the company. Search failed to reveal the ore in the shafts and tunnels, and the inference was that it had been taken out in a surreptitious manner during the night, or at hours when darkness would allow the thieve to remove the ore in small lots without attracting attention.

There was but one remedy for the evil, and that was adopted by the manager. Every employee of the Victor was discharged and the new crew placed under surveillance.

The Victor crew received more than a discharge. As the miners came off shift, the superintendent invited them into his office "for a cigar." They gladly complied, and found themselves looking not at cigars, but down the gun barrels of six hired detectives. The detectives strip-searched the miners, confiscated the high-grade, and had everyone fired—then hauled outside and beaten. The mine operators hired a new crew, but it probably did little good.

High-graders were ingenious, smuggling free gold and rich ores out of the mines in hollow boot heels, tubular pockets sewn into the inside seams of trousers, double inner bands of hats, and unconsumed portions of lunches. Some miners pulverized the ore, mixed it with machine grease, then rubbed it in their hair or on their clothing. High-graders also worked in teams, usually composed of an underground miner and a "toplander." Before miners "sent up" for repair rock drills and pumps, they dismantled and packed them full of highgrade. High-graders even concealed gold in cars of waste rock bound for the dumps; at night, the glow of shrouded lanterns moved eerily across the dumps as miners recovered "their" gold.

Mine owners tried everything to stop the loss of gold. They insisted that workers sack all obviously rich ore under supervision right in the stopes in sturdy, locked canvas bags. Security men established change rooms where miners left their mine clothes then passed naked before inspectors, even stepping over high "jump bars" to show no gold was concealed between their legs. But even that failed to solve the problem, for miners simply hid large quantities of high-grade at specified locations underground, the confidently walked off shift "clean." Then the "nightriders," using old manways and miles of abandoned tunnels, ventured underground at night, recovered the gold and were gone by daylight. But nightriding was a hazardous profession, for the gold recovery didn't always go smoothly. Armed guards waited on the surface, and the nightriders' chances of being injured or becoming lost in the dark underground labyrinths was frighteningly real. Armed guards were sometimes posted in the underground, their lights extinguished, to shoot the nightriders on sight, and the Cripple Creek district had at least two underground shoot-outs.

Much high-grade went to a network of so-called assayers who served "fences" doing little more than purchasing identifiable ores and reducing them down to generic gold bullion, extracting the gold with everything from fire assay materials to dead roast ovens and laboratory chlorination equipment. Fence assaying was a very competitive profession; fences sent agents to courteously collect the day's high-grade from miners' rooms, homes and favorite saloons, and even provided complimentary money belts as smuggling aids. Fences paid $10 to $12 per ounce of contained gold, leaving plenty of room for their own profit. Independent high-graders avoided the middleman, building charcoal-fired dead roast ovens in their backyards. While the men were on shift, wives and children dead roasted calaverite into gleaming beads of metallic gold. After a crude hammer crushing, panning recovered the coarse gold and amalgamation picked up the fine

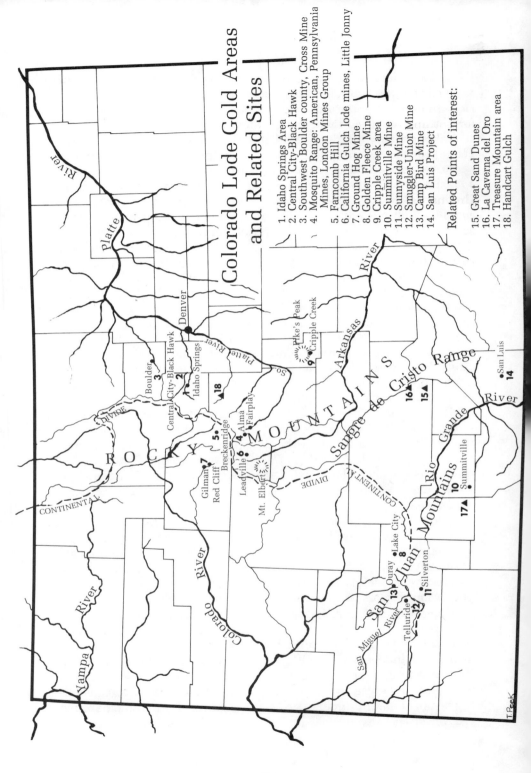

# Colorado Lode Gold Areas and Related Sites

1. Idaho Springs Area
2. Central City-Black Hawk
3. Southwest Boulder county, Cross Mine
4. Mosquito Range: American, Pennsylvania Mines, London Mines Group
5. Farncomb Hill
6. California Gulch lode mines, Little Jonny
7. Ground Hog Mine
8. Golden Fleece Mine
9. Cripple Creek area
10. Summitville Mine
11. Sunnyside Mine
12. Smuggler-Union Mine
13. Camp Bird Mine
14. San Luis Project

Related Points of interest:

15. Great Sand Dunes
16. La Caverna del Oro
17. Treasure Mountain area
18. Handcart Gulch

particles. Whether by the fence or independently, many miners enjoyed an income far above their regular wages. Some of the smaller rich mines never bothered to pay wages. Yet miners lined up to "work for nothing"—taking their pay in what they could high-grade.

Although criminal, high-grading enjoyed broad community support. Merchants knew that gold ore shipped out of the district benefited them only indirectly, and also that much of the money spent so freely in their stores and saloons came directly from high-grading. Unions defended high-graders at every opportunity; even juries, composed largely of merchants and miners—high-graders themselves—had little reason to convict a miner charged with gold theft. A Cripple Creek judge acquitted a high-grader caught red-handed, ruling that "mineral is real estate," and part of the "scenery," and "you can't steal the scenery."

Frustrated mine owners made their strongest stand against high-grading on February 23, 1902. Eight dynamite explosions shattered the nighttime stillness, and when Cripple Creek residents arose, they found eight fence-assay offices blown to bits. But high-grading continued, and mine owners finally received limited relief in 1915 when the state legislature passed a law requiring all assayers to post bonds and record all transactions by name, amount and mine of origin.

High-grading always was "part of the game" at Cripple Creek. How much gold miners high-graded will, of course, never be known. But the best estimates, which may be conservative, point to about $1 million per year over the entire 25-year boom period. On the bottom line, it amounted to one of the greatest gold robberies in history. Cripple Creek miners took home about one million troy ounces— thirty-two standard *tons*—of gold worth $20 million.

Cripple Creek gold was important in bringing a new U.S. Mint to Denver, replacing the old Clark, Gruber & Co. building that had served as a federal assay mint since 1863. Congress made the initial appropriation for a new U.S. Mint in 1895, and competition between four cities soon narrowed to New York and Denver. By the time construction was actually authorized in 1899, the flood of Cripple Creek gold made Denver the logical and overwhelming choice. When the Treasury Department completed its new $800,000 U.S. Mint facility in 1904, the historic Clark, Gruber & Co. building was torn down. In 1906 the minting of gold coins resumed in Denver for the first time in 44 years. The coins were standard U.S. Mint issue and no longer carried the name of "Pike's Peak." Nevertheless, they were "Pike's Peak gold", literally and figuratively, for most of the gold in the gleaming new coins came straight from the booming gold camp of Cripple Creek high on the shoulder of Pike's Peak.

Cripple Creek also helped put the gold on Colorado's capitol dome. Gilding the dome of the planned new capitol building was first proposed by Colorado pioneer Otto Mears in 1890. Mears believed gold would "set off" the capitol architecturally and symbolize the significance of gold in the state's history. But Mears found little support, especially among Colorado's silver barons. When the new capitol building was completed in 1900, the 42-foot-diameter dome was covered with a copper-tin-zinc sheeting. By 1906, however, as Colorado continued to lead the nation in gold production, legislators were far more receptive to Mears' idea. The Colorado Mining Association collected 200 troy ounces of gold from its members and donated it to the state. The dome was first prepared with 7½ tons of thin lead sheet as a base for the film-like leaf of 999 fine gold. When gilding was completed in 1907, Colorado was approaching its fiftieth anniversary of the discovery of gold on the South Platte River, and the value of its cumulative gold production had topped a half billion dollars.

In 1908 Cripple Creek produced another 21 tons of gold worth $13 million. Bob Womack, the man who discovered it all, was bedridden in Colorado Springs, his health gone and just as broke as he was that day eighteen years earlier when he dug his way into the El Paso lode. A friend organized the Bob Womack Relief Fund, which raised $800 to help with his medical expenses. Womack died in 1909, the year Cripple Creek's cumulative production topped $200 million.

The last of chlorination mills closed in 1911, and mine operators used cyanidation on virtually all of the Cripple Creek ores. By that time, ore grades had declined and the deep mines needed expensive drainage tunnels to dewater them. Only 140 of the original 475 mines still operated, but they were larger, more efficient and still eminently profitable. In 1914 Cripple creek was back in the headlines, not for the $12 million of gold produced that year, but for one of the most exciting discoveries in the history of gold mining.

The Cresson Mine was one of Cripple Creek's biggest producers. Mining engineer Dick Roelofs had taken over as superintendent in 1910, increasing profits and pushing exploratory workings down to the 1300 level, 1,300 feet below the surface. On November 24, 1914, miners on the 1200 level blasted into a large geode, a hollow area called a "vug." Miners occasionally encountered vugs in the Cripple Creek underground, many lined with crystals of quartz and fluorite. This one, however, from what little the miners could see, seemed lined with gold. Roelofs was summoned, and after a cursory inspection he realized that this vug was a high-grader's dream. He suspended all mining on the 1200 level, ordered the emplacement of a sturdy steel door, then posted three armed guards.

The next day Roelofs guided one of the mine's owners and an attorney, acting as a witness, down to the 1200 level. Together, they held magnesium flares into the small, crumbling opening leading into the vug. Marshall Sprague later described the scene in *Money Mountain*, his history of Cripple Creek:

> What the three men saw stunned them as a child is stunned by his first Christmas tree. It was cave of sparkling jewels. The brightness blinded them at first but then they made out that the jewels were millions of gold crystals—sylvanite and calaverite. Splattered among the crystals were flowing flakes of pure gold as big as thumbnails. . . .
>
> This was an Arabian Nights scene of the twentieth century.
> . . . This vug was richer than any room in Tiffany's.

Sprague's description, if anything, was understated. On January 2, 1915, *The Engineering and Mining Journal*, a trade publication respected for its objectivity, provided this account of the now-famous "Cresson Vug":

> A visit to the mine and personal inspection of the bonanza impresses one tremendously. . . . The chamber is about 14 feet wide, 23 feet long and 36 feet high. . . .
>
> When first opened the cavity had the appearance of a stope filled with broken ore. The filling consisted of fragments of breccia encrusted and permeated with crystals of sylvanite and calaverite. Most of this material couldn't be mined with a pick. The telluride crystals were of two kinds: some were tabular, many over 3/4 in. long, and many of these exposing a face of not less than 1/2 sq. in.; others were small and thick. Irregular deposits of crumbly, crystalline material thickly encrusted with telluride crystals formed the richest ore and assayed from $10,000 to $16,000 a ton. This material was carefully sacked, together with other fragments which were thickly encrusted with sylvanite. The balance of the chamber filling was shoveled over a 1-in. screen, and undersize assaying from $5,000 to $6,500, and the oversize running from $1,000 to $1,500. After the removal of the bulk of the filling, shots were put into the walls and all of the rock broken down and found filled with sylvanite crystals, as well as the walls from which the material was broken. . . . The net value of the ore actually in sight may be conservatively estimated at not less than $500,000.

79

Even that professional estimate substantially undervalued the ore. Cleaning out the vug took a full month. Miners worked under on-the-spot supervision, filling over 1,400 canvas ore sacks with "scraping" crystals—worth $400,000. "Low grade" material filled another 1,000 sacks—worth $100,000. Only then were miners permitted to drill and blast down the walls—which graded over 50 ounces per ton—eventually turning the vug into a huge, mined-out stope. When the job was done, the Cresson vug had yielded about 60,000 troy ounces—two tons—of gold worth $1.2 million.

Sampling, assaying and treating the Cresson vug ore became almost as big a job as cleaning out the vug itself. Rail shipments of the ore from Cripple Creek were accompanied by shotgun guards, and even rated special mention in *The Engineering and Mining Journal*:

> CRESSON [Cripple Creek]—Shipment of high-grade sent to Copeland sampler Jan. 24, from the now-famous 12th level. Two cars in one lot. 80 tons, of first grade; three cars, 88 tons, of second grade. Entire shipment sampled twice, extra precautions taken for sampling. Average grade $3 per pound; total about one million dollars.

The first grade ores contained 206 troy ounces of gold per ton, the second grade 105 troy ounces. Since the slightest error in sampling or assaying would cost someone tens of thousands of dollars, mine owners and mill operators negotiated for weeks before agreeing on the numbers. Furthermore, the Cresson vug ore was far too rich for any standard extraction process. It first had to be "deriched" before cyanidation, that is, mixed with carefully assayed "mine run" ores to lower the overall grade below 50 ounces per ton before cyanidation.

The Cresson vug gave Cripple Creek world wide publicity, boosted mining stock sales, and generated new interest in the deeper ores below a thousand feet. The hero, of course, was Dick Roelofs, who had taken personal charge of the situation in the critical early hours, then supervised the subsequent mining. He received a huge bonus in cash and stock from the directors of the Cresson Gold Mining and Milling Company, as well as lucrative offers of employment from gold-mining companies all over the West. But Roelofs had spent enough time in dark drifts filled with dynamite fumes; he retired to New York City for a more agreeable life, as he put it, of "wine, women and song."

The Cresson went on to cumulatively produce $49 million, second in Cripple Creek only to the $60 million Portland. These two headed a list of twenty mines producing over $4 million each. The "golden age" of Cripple Creek finally ended in 1918 when the district production dropped below $10 million per year for the first time since 1897. By 1920 just 41 mines were active, and annual production fell to "only" $4.3 million. By that time Cripple Creek had produced over 500 tons of gold worth a third of a billion dollars, ranking second among all gold-producing districts of the world.

*Daughter, I've struck it rich.*
Thomas F. Walsh, to his daughter, Evalyn,
on discovering the Camp Bird Vein, 1896

*We had good ore but, at twenty dollars an ounce, it
wasn't worth mining it.*
Gus Seppi, Leadville miner, on gold mining in 1928

# 5

# $20 GOLD: FROM BONANZA TO BUST
## 1896-1929

Although Cripple Creek dominated Colorado's gold production in the late 1890s, the San Juan mines had hit their peak, contributing nearly four million ounces per year. The leading producers were the Golden Fleece, the Sunnyside and the three big mines of San Miguel County—the Smuggler-Union, the Tomboy and the Liberty Bell. By 1920, those three mines had combined to produce over a hundred tons of gold worth $60 million, ranking San Miguel third among all of Colorado's gold-producing counties.

The big San Juan deposits discovered in the mid-1870s were now all developed, except one—the vein six miles southeast of Ouray in Imogene Basin, staked in 1877 by those two English prospectors, William Weston and George Barber. Although Weston and Barber found only low-grade copper-silver-lead mineralization in the discovery claims, the Gertrude and the Una, they still managed to sell them for $40,000 to the Allied Mines Company in 1881. Allied Mines planned a 50-foot-long crosscut to intersect the vein on the Gertrude claim, but cut only 38 feet before the high-country winter halted exploration work. Allied Mines fell into bankruptcy in 1883, again suspending work. The last twelve feet of the crosscut were finally driven in 1884, apparently to fulfill patent requirements. In one of the great mistakes of Colorado mining, those last twelve feet were never properly sampled. Nothing more would be done with the prospects in Imogene Basin until the arrival of Thomas Walsh in 1896.

Thomas F. Walsh was born in Ireland, immigrated to the United States at age nineteen, worked briefly as a carpenter in New England, then headed west following the tales of gold and silver in Colorado. From Central City he joined the 1876 gold rush to the Black Hills of Dakota Territory, returning to Denver with $75,000 earned in placer mining and carpentry. Walsh then moved to Leadville, invested his capital wisely, married, and had a daughter and son. He next moved into smelting, but his timing was poor. His investments fell apart in the silver market crash of 1893, and Walsh went quickly from employer to employee.

Walsh moved on to Silverton, where he found work as a smelter manager and part-time prospector, searching specifically for low-grade, high-silica base metal ores suitable as a smelting flux. By 1896 Walsh was living in Ouray; although nearly broke, he continued prospecting and picking up claims for back taxes, usually silver-copper-lead claims that sold dirt-cheap after the silver crash. His acquisitions included the old Gertrude and Una claims in 11,500-foot-high Imogene Basin. Walsh was unable to even enter the old exploratory crosscut; over the years of inactivity, repetitive snow-slides had covered the portal and compacted it into a perpetual alpine snowfield. But he did search through the old mine dumps 300 feet below the portal, finding what looked like gold-bearing rock. Assays confirmed gold, but only about one-tenth of an ounce per ton.

Walsh next scraped up some money to hire a miner to tunnel through the snow and ice to sample the old crosscut. Assay returns showed low-grade lead-copper-zinc, leaving him puzzled by the gold values in the dump. Although sick with fever, Walsh climbed to Imogene Basin to personally inspect the fourteen-year-old crosscut. He found the vein that had produced the copper-lead-zinc samples; directly adjacent to it lay a three-foot-thick vein of seemingly barren quartz. Looking closer, Walsh discerned tiny specks of blackish crystalline mineral. Thinking it might be some type of telluride, he used the last of his strength to pack down a sack of samples, leaving them for assay. He still lay sick in bed when the results came back. Walsh read them quietly several times, then summoned his six-year-old daughter, Evalyn, to his side.

"You must keep a secret I'm going to tell you, promise?"

"Yes, Papa."

"Daughter, I've struck it rich."

During the next two months, Walsh quietly bought or staked all the open ground near the vein. By the time he allowed word of the strike to spread, he had eliminated cause for a gold rush to Imogene Basin. Just as Harry Farncomb had done at Farncomb Hill at Breckenridge in 1879, Walsh controlled everything in sight. Walsh took no partners and sold no shares. Using his assay reports that estimated the gold content of the ores as high as three thousand dollars per ton and his uncontested control of the property, he borrowed development capital.

By 1897 work on the Camp Bird Mine, named for the gray jay, the familiar high country "camp robber," progressed on three levels, with an 11,000-foot-long aerial tramway to the lower mill. To make the mine and mill self-sufficient even during the long, snowy winters, Walsh constructed a self-contained community that included a three-story boardinghouse, shops and warehouses, all steam-heated and lit with electricity. In February 1898 the twenty-stamp mill and amalgamation-concentration plant began operation. The Camp Bird Mine

*A section of the 11,000-foot-long aerial tramway that connected the Camp Bird Mine with the lower mill. Miners routinely rode the swinging one-ton ore buckets to and from work.*
—Colorado Historical Society

*The Number 3 Level of Thomas F. Walsh's Camp Bird Mine. An elevation of about 11,500 feet meant difficult working conditions during the long alpine winter. By 1916, the Camp Bird had produced 32 tons of gold.*
—Colorado Historical Society

began full production by 1899, with an expanded forty-stamp mill crushing 200 tons of high-grade ore every day.

Decades later, Evalyn Walsh McLean recalled those exciting years. "The Camp Bird Mine was producing $5,000 a day in profits," Thomas Walsh's daughter wrote. "Each morning we Walshes arose richer than we had gone to bed. Mine and mill ran day and night."

By 1902 the mine had produced almost 200,000 ounces of gold—about six tons—worth $4 million, a record 60 percent of which—$2.4 million—was clear profit. Since Thomas Walsh had no debts, no partners and no stockholders, the Camp Bird is considered the biggest, richest gold mine ever owned by an individual. But Walsh soon had enough of gold mining and in 1902 sold the Camp Bird to a British investment group, Camp Bird, Ltd., for $3.5 million in cash, $500,000 in shares, and future royalties of $2 million on ore reserves yet unproven. Walsh built a magnificent mansion in Washington, D. C. and moved easily into the top levels of society, regularly entertaining presidents and European nobility. By the time of his death in 1910, Walsh had personally realized at least $8 million from the Camp Bird. His daughter, Evalyn, gained international notoriety as a wealthy but troubled heiress, using part of the Camp Bird fortune to purchase the Hope Diamond.

*The capitol dome reflects brilliantly with the rich luster of gold for a good reason—it is gold. The original gold, 200 troy ounces of it, was donated by members of the Colorado Mining Association and placed on the dome in 1907. Historically, Colorado could not have chosen a more appropriate medium to decorate its capitol.*

*Obverse and reverse of $20 gold piece minted in Denver in 1860 by Clark, Gruber & Co.* —From the collection of the Colorado History Museum, courtesy of The Colorado Historical Society

# Colorado Placer Gold

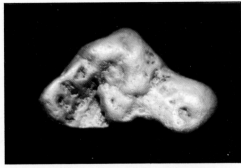

*1. The "Penn Hill" nugget weighs 11.95 troy ounces and is the largest Colorado placer nugget known to exist.* —The Denver Museum of Natural History

*2. The "Turtle Nugget" weighs 8 troy ounces and is the second largest known Colorado placer nugget. It was mined at Pennsylvania Mountain in 1990.* —The Denver Museum of Natural History

*3. A three-troy ounce gold nugget from Fairplay.* —The Bowman Collection, courtesy of the National Mining Hall of Fame & Museum

*4. Colorado placer gold in small nuggets and coarse flakes. From upper Arkansas River and Cache Creek area.*

## *Colorado Lode Gold*  5

6

5. *"Tom's Baby," from Farncomb Hill near Breckenridge, is the largest mass of crystallized gold known to have been mined in Colorado. It weighs 102 troy ounces and measures approximately eight inches in length.* —From the John F. Campion Collection, now displayed at the Denver Museum of Natural history

6. *Gold-in-quartz from Idaho Spring's Humboldt Mine. Specimen is 5.0 inches long.* —From the Bowman Collection, courtesy of the National Mining Hall of Fame & Museum

7. *This superb "ram's horn" is the world's largest known specimen of wire gold. Mined at the Ground Hog Mine, Eagle County in 1887, it weighs 8 troy ounces, and measures five inches in length and an inch in diameter at the base.* —From the collection of the Harvard Minerological Museum

8. *Crystalized gold from Leadville's Little Jonny Mine. It weighs 24 troy ounces and measures 4.5 inches in length.* —From the Bowman Collection, courtesy of the National Mining Hall of Fame & Museum

7

8

9. *The cyanide leach pad at the modern Summitville open pit mine in the late 1980s.*

10. *The Summitville "gold boulder" weighs 81.43 pounds avoirdupois; one-fifth of its weight is gold (about 316 troy ounces).*

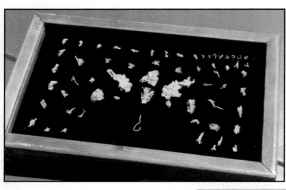

11. *A private collection of crystallized gold from Farncomb Hill near Breckenridge.*

12. *This doré bar poured by Summitville Consolidated Mining Co. in 1988 is 85 percent gold and weighs about 900 troy ounces (about 61 pounds avoirdupois).*

Camp Bird, Ltd. enjoyed continued success, despite a disaster in 1906. Avalanches had always plagued mining in the high elevations of the steep San Juan Mountains. When a series of slides blocked the Animas Canyon route of the Denver & Rio Grande Railroad in 1887, only two trains got through in ninety days. Avalanches had repeatedly damaged the Smuggler-Union's aerial tramway, and in 1902 eighteen men were killed at the Liberty Bell when a slide swept away the mill and much of the tramway. On March 16, 1906, the Camp Bird's turn came. T. A. Rickard, in *Across the San Juan Mountains*, described the tragedy.

> For a number of days the snow had fallen, so that a thick covering of new snow lay on the smooth frozen surface of the winter. Starting high on Mt. Hayden, the slide first upset thirteen towers of the tramway and then, leaping over a high cliff, it wrecked several warehouses and coal sheds before striking the mill itself. Before coming to rest, it crushed the lower story of a bunk-house, devoted to a reading room, endangering the lives of seven men, who were rescued comparatively unhurt. As earlier slides on the same day had broken the wires that transmitted electric power, the mill happened to be idle and only three men were in it. One was unhurt, though entangled in the wreckage; a second was dug out from under three feet of snow and timbers, also only slightly bruised; the third was killed. The avalanche made no noise save when the timbers of the mill cracked, but the air was quickly laden with a mist of snow. The particular slide that did the damage was known, that is, its path in previous springs was marked by a lane in the forest above the mill, but it had never been known to run so far or to be so violent.

More trouble was still to come; three days later, fire consumed the mill ruins and the boiler house. In the amalgamation plant, the intense heat had evaporated the mercury from the big copper recovery plates, leaving the copper thickly gold-plated and the floor littered with large masses of dirty gold sponge. Camp Bird, Ltd., rebuilt immediately, expanding the mill to sixty stamps and installing a cyanidation circuit to extract gold from the lower grade ores and tailings. By 1916 Camp Bird, Ltd. had produced over one million ounces—32 tons—of gold, along with large quantities of silver, copper and lead, earning a clear profit of $15 million.

In 1900, when Colorado hit its all-time record annual gold production of 1.4 million troy ounces worth $28 million, lode mining accounted for virtually all of it. The estimated annual production of the state's placers had fallen to only 4,000 ounces, worth a mere $80,000. Four decades of sluicing, ground sluicing and hydraulicking had depleted most of the better gravels. If Colorado placer mining had a future, it rested in the large volumes of gold-bearing gravels that lay below the water table.

Diverting an entire stream flow provided placer miners only limited access to the lower gravels. The first mechanical means these miners had to exploit deep gravels was the hydraulic elevator, which was tried on Clear Creek near Golden in 1886. Hydraulic elevators were huge, stationary suction devices. Like regular hydraulic monitors, they required a large supply of water under a head of several hundred feet. Under great pressure, the water was directed through a venturi-type fitting atop a long, heavy, steel pipe two or three feet in diameter, the base of which was deeply immersed in underwater gravels. The venturi effect created a powerful suction, drawing mud, silt, sand, gravel and even boulders up the length of the pipe, and spewing it all onto the surface where it was washed through sluices.

By 1900 three hydraulic elevators operated in Summit County, two near Breckenridge and one at Dillon, all with limited success. By far the most ambitious project was that of the Gold Pan Company, which constructed a three-mile-long diversion ditch and an 8,000-foot-long pipeline to deliver water under a 350-foot head to four big hydraulic elevators just south of Breckenridge. The company began in 1903; within a year, the gaping, flooded Gold Pan pit was down seventy-three feet to bedrock, encountering more trouble than gold. The grades of the deep gravels, never properly tested, were lower than the operators had hoped, and three-foot-diameter boulders frequently plugged and damaged the elevator pipes. With operating costs far greater than the value of the recovered gold, the Gold Pan pit shut down in 1905, the biggest—and last—of Colorado's hydraulic elevators.

Ben Stanley Revett, the British mining engineer who had managed the profitable hydraulicking operation at Cache Creek near Granite in the mid-1880s, had his eye on the gold hidden in the deep placers. Revett became superintendent of the Wapiti Mine, one of John F. Campion's Farncomb Hill properties at Breckenridge, in 1889. But with his heart still in placer mining, he soon left for Idaho's Salmon River goldfields. By 1897 Revett was back in Breckenridge, determined to work the deep gravels of the Swan and Blue rivers with a new method—the floating bucketline dredge recently developed in the New Zealand goldfields. The first floating bucketline dredge in the U.S. had just started work at Bannack, Montana, and Revett planned to have the second working in Colorado.

Revett's first challenge was determing if the gold content of the deep gravels warrented the big investment in a dredge. His first

*Ben Stanley Revett's Reliance beginning operations at the confluence of French Gulch and the Blue River near Breckenridge in 1905. The Reliance was the first floating bucketline dredge powerful enough to successfully work Colorado's deep placer gravels.* —Colorado Historical Society

effort, a sixty-foot-deep shaft to bedrock in the Swan River channel, failed because of flooding. He then tried a churn-type oil-well drill, the first use of such equipment in placer prospecting in Colorado. Although the churn drill produced a mud, rather than a solid core that showed specific strata, it gave a general idea of deep-gravel gold content. Encouraged by the results, Revett set up the North American Gold Dredging Company, found the backing of a Boston investment group, and ordered two "New Zealand-type" dredges from a San Francisco ironworks. By the time Revett had the components manufactured, shipped, assembled and put into operation on the lower Swan River in 1898, his dredges were the third and fourth to operate in the United States. But Revett found both incapable of handling big boulders and tightly compacted deep gravels. Within a year he dismantled them and replaced them with two others that offered little improvement. Competition appeared in 1899 when the Blue River Gold Excavating Company launched two of their own "gold boats," which proved as unsuccessful as Revett's.

93

The unauspicious beginning of the "Breckenridge Navy" made Revett more determined than ever to mine the deep gravels. In 1904 he founded the Reliance Dredging Company, pouring $90,000 into the steam-powered Reliance, a much heavier dredge of his own design. With the voracious appetite of 3,000 cubic yards of gravel per day, the Reliance became Colorado's first successful floating bucketline dredge. Working near the mouth of French Gulch, it recovered sixty ounces of placer gold per day and netted $50,000 in its first seven-month season. In 1908 Revett modified the Reliance for year-round operation, quite a feat in the hard winters at an elevation of 9,400 feet. Steam heated the dredge interior to keep the sluices from freezing, and also thawed the rock-hard, frozen gravels ahead of the gouging bucketline. More improvements came in 1909 when Revett had the Reliance converted from steam to electric power, reducing its basic operating costs.

Ben Stanley Revett's Reliance proved that Colorado placer mining still had a future. Soon, five dredges operated at Breckenridge, with others gouging and washing gravels on lower Clear Creek in Jefferson County, Beaver Creek near Hahn's Peak in Routt County, Willow Creek in Gunnison County, Lay and Timberlake creeks in Moffat County, the South Platte River near Fairplay in Park County, Placer Creek in old Grayback District in Costilla County, and Box Creek in Lake County. By 1916 Colorado's estimated placer-gold production soared to 40,000 ounces, worth nearly three-quarters of a million dollars—the highest annual placer production since the great days of the Pike's Peak rush.

The Derry dredge, working Box Creek at the base of Mt. Elbert in Lake County, was typical of the second generation of floating bucketline dredges. Manufactured by the New York Engineering Company of Yonkers, New York, the dredge began operation in 1915 under the banner of the Empire Gold Dredging Company. The dredge had a 120-foot-long wooden hull, and an overall length of 300 feet. A long boom supporting a continuous 28-bucket dragline extended forward, suspended on cables from an overhead steel tower. In operation, the bucketline gouged its way forward into the channel, scooping five cubic yards of gravel in each bucket and conveying it inside the dredge for sorting. The dredge channeled finer sands and gravels through a long steel sluice with mercury-filled riffles; the coarse tailings, mainly cobbles and boulders, were carried out the rear of the dredge on a 75-foot-long conveyor-stacker and dumped in heaps.

The lake on which the dredge floated actually moved; the dredge dug it out from the front and filled in from the rear. Over several

*Maintenance and repair of the bucketline and sleeve bearings took most of a dredge crew's time. Shown is the bucketline of a Breckenridge dredge about 1916.* —Colorado Historical Society

years, the dredge "sailed" about two miles back and forth over the broad channel of Box Creek. Although the buckets and sleeve bearings were made of hard manganese steel, constant immersion in fine quartz sand took its toll and the 25-man crew spent most of their time on maintenance and repair. Their biggest job was replacing worn-out bearings and shear pins that were designed to break whenever boulders jammed the bucketline.

The Derry dredge's first two months of operation were its best. Working in good gravels to a depth of thirty feet, it gouged out and washed 150,000 cubic yards of "dirt," recovering 3,500 ounces of raw placer gold worth nearly $70,000. But the gravel grades it worked soon declined from fifty cents per cubic yard to about twenty cents and its profits declined. The gravel-gold ratio was then about two hundred to one, meaning the dredge had to dig and wash two hundred cubic yards of gravel to recover a single ounce of gold. Its last few years were, at best, a break-even operation. Facing higher operating costs and declining gold recovery, the owners of the Derry dredge dismantled it in 1926 and shipped it to Central America to begin a new career on better dirt.

Cache Creek Park, six miles below Box Creek on the Arkansas River, was one of Colorado's many placer districts ill-suited for the floating bucketline dredges that still managed to survive. In 1894, when profits of the British-owned Twin Lake Hydraulic Gold Mining Syndicate, Ltd. declined, the company was reorganized as Twin Lakes Placers, Ltd. and $100,000 put into expanding the vital water diversion ditch system. By the turn of the century, Twin Lakes Placers continued hydraulicking only on its best ground, leasing most of the Cache Creek property to an army of small companies and independent miners. About two-hundred placer miners worked on Cache Creek, or nearby on the Arkansas River and Lake Creek—and every one of them knew Henry Schutz, proprietor of the Granite General Store in the little town of Granite.

Henry Schutz emigrated from Germany in 1870, working briefly in the Midwest to save the money necessary to journey by covered wagon to Colorado the following year. He became a placer miner, and a good one, making a respectable living washing gold from the well-worked gravels of Clear Creek, the South Platte River at Fairplay and, finally, California Gulch. When he became a naturalized United States citizen in 1881, he opened a general store in Granite. Schutz did well during the hydraulicking days of the 1880s. But, as independent lease mining became more prevalent on Cache Creek, he realized that in the interests of both his business and placer mining, he would have to be more than a merchant.

Over the years Schutz worked as a county doctor, banker and legal advisor to many miners, and when a miner's luck and pay dirt ran out, the advice from his peers was most often, "Talk to Henry." Schutz grubstaked no one, but he did dispense provisions to men whom he knew as hard workers, even though his payment would come "in the next clean-up." Schutz may have been one of the last merchants in Colorado to routinely take dust and small nuggets in trade. When he had the time, Schutz took his gold pans back to the creeks, teaching his sons, Herman and Charles, the fine points of placer mining. Through family mining and trade at the general store, Henry Schutz amassed an extensive collection of small nuggets from Cache Creek Park.

96

Hydraulicking, since it first began at Cache Creek Park under direction of Ben Stanley Revett in 1886, had polluted the Arkansas River with mud and silt. Domestic and agricultural downstream water users finally had enough. In 1910 they won a state court order putting an end to twenty-five years of hydraulic mining in Cache Creek Park. Mining continued with old ground-sluicing methods which, while less water intensive and polluting, were less productive.

Immediately after the hydraulicking injunction, mining in Cache Creek Park was further changed by events spawned by the onset of World War I. As early as 1912, political unrest in Europe began undermining British money markets. When war was declared in August 1914, the British government, under authority of the Defence of the Realms Act, prohibited export of the pound beyond the United Kingdom. This prohibition barred the British backers of Twin Lakes Placers, Ltd. from supporting the operations in Cache Creek Park. By 1916 Twin Lakes Placers, Ltd. had fallen far behind on its tax obligations, and the Cache Creek Park property was put up for tax sale. Ownership, for the first time in thirty years, passed back to American hands.

Hardrock mining, too, changed considerably after the turn of the century. Hardrock metal mining became a trade-off of declining ore grades and technological advancement in both mining and milling methods. Underground safety standards rose, and electric power greatly improved underground lighting, ventilation and hauling. Two other developments also profoundly affected mining and milling—the diamond core drill and the flotation concentration process.

Core-drilling, the taking of solid rock core samples with a diamond-tipped, hollow steel drill, enormously aided mineral exploration. Miners no longer had to drive costly drifts, hoping blindly to intersect unseen veins or ore bodies. Analysis of core sections several hundred feet in length allowed miners to accurately estimate reserves as well as establish more efficient, systematic mining programs. One of the first mines in the United States to use core-drilling was Leadville's Little Jonny in 1894. Although the early core-drill sections, especially when joined in long "strings," had a frustrating tendency to break at the joints, the results at the Little Jonny were spectacular. By 1905 mine owners had made core-drilling their standard method of underground exploration, especially for mines pursuing erratic, vein-type deposits.

The declining ore grades coming out of mines after 1900 meant that direct smelting ores had become rare; most metal ores mined after the turn of the century required concentration before being further treated. The Sunnyside Mine had experimented in concen-

*Leadville's Little Jonny Mine about 1916. Little Jonny was one of the first mines to employ core drilling for underground exploration. Drilling revealed a large body of high grade gold ore, and Little Jonny became one of Colorado's top gold producers about the turn of the century.* —Colorado Historical Society

tration in 1890, and the Wilfley table, a vibrating channeled table that separated dry, crushed ores by specific gravity, was developed in 1895. Mill concentration took a big step forward when the flotation separation process was developed in the early 1900s. In this process low-grade ores were crushed to a fine sand, then mixed into a water slurry. Mill workers then added chemicals, usually light oils or glycerides, and agitated and aerated the entire mixture in vats. Mineral particles adhered to the rising bubbles, forming a mineral-laden froth that was easily separated, dried into a rich concentrate, and shipped to smelters. With the decline of Cripple Creek, gold production in Colorado became increasingly dependent upon by-product and co-product recovery in the mining and milling of low-grade silver and base metal ores. And flotation separation greatly aided silver, lead, zinc and copper mining.

In 1916 the World War I base-metal mining boom peaked, carrying Colorado's gold production over one million ounces one more time. But that was the last million-ounce year Colorado's gold miners ever enjoyed. By 1922 gold production had plummeted to only 300,000 ounces, the lowest annual output since 1892, when development began at Cripple Creek. The hard times were just beginning, for the 1920s were one of the darkest decades in Colorado mining history.

Base metals were beset by low prices in a post-war depression, but gold faced a special problem as a monetary metal. Since 1837 the government had held the price of gold at a fixed $20.67 per troy ounce. But decades of economic inflation had eroded the real purchasing power of the metal; while gold remained at $20.67 per ounce, the cost of labor, materials and services had increased steadily. Post-war inflation then drove the cost of mining to record levels. "$20 gold," as miners called it, while a bonanza during the frontier era, had little glitter left.

Without question, the most exciting event in gold mining in the dismal 1920s took place in Summitville, the forgotten 11,300-foot-high camp in the San Juan Mountains of Rio Grande county. Summitville, Colorado's leading gold district of the early 1880s, now had a new distinction: It was the highest ghost town on the continent. Most mines remained boarded up after the depression of 1893, and no one expected another bonanza at Summitville, especially in the year 1926. More remarkable than the glittering vein of "picture rock" itself was the fact that a miner named Jack Pickens had kept it a secret for eighteen years.

John W. Pickens left his native Tennessee at the age of twenty-four, arriving in Colorado just as Cripple Creek was booming in 1893. Perhaps Pickens found too much excitement in Cripple Creek, for he quickly moved on to Summitville, which already had its best years behind it. Nevertheless, Pickens stayed, for a while earning his living by working for Eugene A. Reynolds, who controlled most of the Summitville mining properties through the Reynolds Mining Company. After many years of unsuccessful prospecting and working for day wages, Pickens' luck took a sudden turn for the better. On a July morning in 1908, Pickens was walking to work along a trail that passed below the Little Annie properties. Noticing an interesting rock in the jumble of talus, he stopped for a closer look and was stunned to find the richest piece of gold ore he had ever seen.

That piece of float gold could have originated only in one place— straight up the steep mountainside. Days later, when no one appeared to be looking, Pickens climbed up to a protruding column of rock. There, overgrown with lichen and partially covered with debris and pine boughs, was a vein of gleaming picture rock that, somehow, in thirty years of mining, had been overlooked. But the moment for Pickens was bittersweet. As a prospector, Pickens felt elated over his find, but he had yet to strike it rich. Reporting the strike would be futile, for others had already claimed or patented all the ground in Summitville.

His most obvious tack to take would be to lease the property, but that, too, he knew would be difficult. The land was controlled by Eugene Reynolds, with whom Pickens had just had a bitter falling out over a petty lawsuit. And Reynolds had vowed to have no further dealings whatever with Pickens, who was now married and living twenty miles away in Del Norte. Pickens returned every summer to inspect his little cabin and, more importantly, to assure himself that no one had stumbled on "his" strike. On one visit, he was appalled to find that a geology class on a field trip from The Colorado School of Mines had set up camp in Summitville. For three weeks, the professor and his students scoured the face of South Mountain, taking samples from every place imaginable and passing perilously close to the vein. Pickens watched them work, afraid to breathe; when the class had loaded the last wagon with samples and equipment and had begun its departure, he almost fainted with relief.

Over the years he tried to get others to lease the property for him. But Reynolds new that Jack Pickens was somehow involved, and his answer was always a flat, no. The irony of it gnawed at Pickens; with a big family to support he was always short of money, yet he had accomplished what most prospectors only dream of. And, while his patience was admirable, he knew he wasn't getting any younger.

When Pickens turned fifty-two in 1921 he saw his first glimmer of hope. Eugene Reynolds died, leaving everything to his daughter, Anna R. Morse. Her husband, Bradish Morse, became the sole administrator of the Reynolds estate, and Pickens knew Morse was well-acquainted with District Judge Jesse Wiley. In what was probably his last chance, Pickens put his full trust in the judge.

The services of Judge Wiley didn't come cheap; he demanded a half-interest in the venture but was able to secure a five-year lease on forty-five claims in the name of the Summitville Gold Mining Company. When Pickens had taken care of the contracts and signed all the details and his dream of eighteen years about to become reality, he broke down in tears.

Pickens waited to disclose the exact location of his vein outcrop to Wiley until July 1927. Wiley, and everyone else now involved in the venture, were incredulous over learning that the vein lay smack in the middle of the original, intensely mined Little Annie claims—and that several old crosscuts had missed it, literally, by inches. *The Denver Post* printed this description of the vein on December 15, 1927:

> . . . the shoot was about twelve feet by twelve feet and went almost straight down with the picture values in a center core

from one foot to two and one-half feet wide right through the twelve feet of shoot. The whole shoot is good shipping ore but that two foot core is simply a wonder.

Jack Pickens indulged in some wild promotion—he had certainly earned the right—claiming Summitville would once again become one of Colorado's leading gold districts. But his discovery, while rich, was small. The Summitville Gold Mining Company went straight for the picture rock core. Mined and sacked by hand, it amounted to only 22 tons. But, grading a phenomenal 230 troy ounces of gold per ton, it returned over $100,000. When the vein was mined out, only 864 tons of ore had been shipped. The overall average grade, however, was 28 ounces per ton, and the return fell just short of a half-million dollars. Jack Pickens bought a fine house in Del Norte, finally taking care of his family the way he had always wanted to. He died in 1933, but for the last six years of his life, rejoiced in knowing that he, too, after all those years of frustration, had struck it rich.

In the 1920s few other Colorado gold miners shared in Jack Pickens' good fortune. Gold became more undervalued each year; by 1928 Colorado's annual production had dropped to only 200,000 ounces, about the same level as the 1870s. With all but one of the big floating bucketline dredges idle, placer mining had all but stopped, with annual placer production estimated at 1,000 ounces or less—an all-time low.

Hardrock mining fared little better. Base metal prices remained depressed, and few mine owners were willing to take the financial risk of operation. With few jobs available, miners who needed work often could only lease sections of older mines and take their chances. In 1928 Leadville miner Gus Seppi was sixteen years old and working with his father in a leased section of the Fanny Rawlings. In its heyday in the 1890s, the Fanny Rawlings was touted as "almost as good as the Little Jonny." But, by 1928 its heyday was long past.

"That was the hardest work I ever did," Seppi recalled many years later. "We'd go down before the sun came up, and come up after the sun went down. We tried everything, but it was a losing battle, even though there was an ounce a ton in some of that ore. I think that was the saddest part. We had good ore but, at twenty dollars an ounce, it wasn't worth mining it."

*The gold rush days of 1858 have returned to the Platte River bottoms. With pick and shovel, sluice box and pan, prospectors are seeking gold. . .*

—*The New York Times,* March 13, 1932

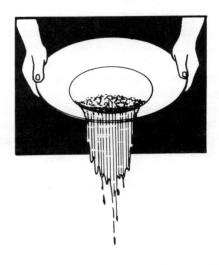

# 6

# $35 GOLD:
# TOO LITTLE, TOO LATE
## 1930 – 1969

The stock market crash of 1929 marked the beginning of the Great Depression, the economic collapse that hastened the inevitable revaluation of gold. By 1932 a growing bank run on gold reflected the public's lack of confidence in the United States paper currency. The drain on federal gold reserves soon brought proposals to repeal the Gold Standard Act. An upward revaluation of gold against the dollar seemed certain, and the only questions were when and how much. Anticipation of higher gold prices had already spurred renewed investment and speculation in gold, gold mining and gold-mining properties.

One of the first signs of a rebirth of gold mining in Colorado occurred in the place it all began seventy-four years earlier—the South Platte River. Amid the growing unemployment of 1931, a few dozen of Denver's many jobless citizens appeared on the banks of the South Platte, gold pans and shovels in hand. They at first found themselves the butt of jokes and newspaper cartoons—"Excuse me, sir, but aren't you seventy years too late?" But the jokes stopped abruptly when the Denver Mint confirmed that it had purchased some of their placer gold, in the usual two troy-ounce minimum lots. The following spring, hundreds flocked down to the banks of the South Platte River within the city limits of Denver, Englewood and

Littleton, and *The New York Times* reported the "rush" on March 13, 1932:

ANOTHER PLATTE GOLD RUSH

DENVER, March 9.—The gold rush days of 1858 have returned to the Platte River bottoms. With pick and shovel, sluice box and pan, prospectors are seeking gold in the mud flats. The miners represent many types and most of them depend upon their daily diggings for capital. Some average a dollar day while the best placer mine turns out $7 in gold and often garnets worth several dollars are found. Men and women work in the mining camp.

That gold remained in the historic "Cherry Creek diggings" surprised many Denver area residents. And, while a dollar a day wasn't a fortune, it was a dollar that many couldn't earn elsewhere. Small-scale placer mining suddenly emerged as a logical constructive outlet for the energies of the legion of unemployed. When veteran placer miners noted that "half of 'em didn't know which side of the pan was up," municipal officials decided it was worth teaching them. The South Platte River found its way back into *The New York Times* a few weeks later in an Associated Press article about the "gold schools":

*A gold panning school being conducted on the banks of the South Platte River in Denver in 1932. Denver's gold panning schools were an effort to create jobs during the Depression years and received national attention.*
—Colorado Historical Society

*An old-time Colorado gold miner teaches the secrets of gold panning to a young woman at one of Denver's gold panning schools on the banks of the South Platte River.* —Colorado Historical Society

## DENVER IDLE LEARN TO PAN GOLD
## IN SOUTH PLATTE RIVER SCHOOL

DENVER, May 21.—Chiefly as a measure to relieve unemployment, several Colorado cities are conducting schools for gold diggers. The latest opened this week in Denver under the auspices of Mayor George D. Begole, the Vocational Training Department and mining men.

With half a dozen experienced placer miners in charge, forty sluice boxes have been installed in the South Platte River, within the city limits, and within a few hundred feet of the spot where gold was first discovered in Colorado by W. Green Russell and his party of Georgia and Cherokee miners.

Almost continuously since the first discovery of these sands, they have been worked every Spring and Summer by miners with gold pan and sluice box, who have reported making from $1.50 to $2 per day.

The new gold fever was just beginning in Colorado. The United States went off the Gold Standard on April 9, 1933; the Treasury Department immediately ceased gold coinage, recalled all gold coins in circulation, banned the export of gold, and restricted private ownership of the metal. In a quasi-free market after ninety-six years at $20.67 per troy ounce, the price of gold began to rise. Gold mining shares rose on the stock exchanges, and in towns including Central City, Breckenridge and Fairplay, the old-timers rummaged through sheds and garages in search of the dented gold pans and rusted shovels. With the lure of gold nearly as strong as it was back in the days of '59, prospectors again headed into the gulches and hills. The raging gold fever made wild rumors of bonanza strikes inevitable. This story, completely unsubstantiated, made *The New York Times* and many other newspapers on the Associated Press wire:

COLORADO GOLD RUSH STARTED BY "STRIKE"

TENT CITY RISES AT GULCH WHERE NEGRO
FOUND PAY DIRT, AND AUTOS BY DOZEN JOIN

CANON CITY, Col., May 13 (AP).—Deep mountain gulches which for years had echoed nothing but the howls of night-prowling animals resounded today with picks and shovels.

Bearded veteran prospectors and tenderfeet jostled on the rock-strewn road into the upper Copper Gulch country where yesterday a Negro prospector, Robert Hoard, found "pay dirt" which runs $38 to the ton.

His discovery started a gold stampede. By the time Hoard had grown calm, more than 250 automobiles loaded with men and women had reached the gulch country. A tent city sprang up overnight. Claims were staked for miles around. Squabbles over overlapping claims and claim jumping added to the excitement.

Dozens of other automobiles, some modern, others of antique vintage, were headed for the winding mountain road, as meager reports of smaller strikes came back to this city.

Coincident with Hoard's announcement, Ed Hollister, state prison fingerprint expert; James Mow, hardrock miner; and John Drake, a school teacher, displayed samples of gold ore which contained $500 gold to the ton.

The traces of gold found in upper Copper Gulch had been grandly exaggerated in the retelling. The biggest excitement of the "Copper Gulch rush" was probably the fights that broke out over right-of-way in a four-mile-long traffic jam involving automobiles, trucks and horse-drawn wagons.

The rise in the price of gold overshadowed such disappointments: gold first hit $25 per troy ounce, then $30 by the end of 1933, and interest in Colorado gold spread beyond the state lines. "Quite a few people came up here from Kansas and Oklahoma," recalled Leadville miner Gus Seppi. "Clear Creek had squatters on it from one end to the other, whole families living in tents and beat-up trucks, panning and shoveling dirt into sluices all day long. Most of them were trespassing on claims and private land, and the sheriffs were busy throwing them off. Trying to wash out a little gold was better than sitting home starving."

On January 30, 1934 the Department of the Treasury again fixed the price of gold, this time at $35 per troy ounce. Many believed that the level was temporary, and that gold would hit $50 or even $60 per troy ounce within a year. Prospectors staked gold claims—both lode and placer—in numbers unheard of since the 1890s. With more people looking for gold, more gold was being found, some of it in unlikely places, as reported in *The New York Times* in March 1934:

### GOLD IN DENVER STREETS

DENVER, Mar. 22.—Denver streets and alleys may be paved with high-grade gold ore, it developed recently. Many of the streets are paved with smelter slag. This slag was assayed recently and showed values running up to $1,100 a ton in gold silver. City officials are investigating to determine if assays indicate general or isolated values. If the former it is possible that the next CWA project here will be the prospecting of Denver streets.

That report started a rush to assay mine dumps, mill wastes and smelter slag all over Colorado. One of the biggest "strikes" was made on the old Leadville smelter slags that the Denver & Rio Grande Western Railroad had long used as a cheap, heavy rail bed ballast. Some assays on the slag ballast showed hundreds of dollars of gold and silver per ton. One "prospector" calculated—and informed the newspapers—that every mile of single-track rail bed contained millions of dollars worth of gold and silver. As smelter men smiled and cautioned that extracting gold from the heavy, high-iron slags would be costly, the railroad issued public warnings that removing rail-bed ballast could create serious safety hazards.

While $35 gold had its first and most visible effects on the Depression-era unemployed fortune hunters and dreamers, it ultimately had its greatest effect in reviving the depressed Colorado gold-mining industry. Although many miners still prayed for the government to turn gold loose toward $60 per troy ounce, investment capital loosened, some mines reopened, and gold output climbed for the first time in thirty years. The revival of gold mining in Colorado made *The New York Times* in a feature article in September 1934:

### GOLD FEVER GROWS IN COLORADO AREA

#### PRACTICAL MINING MEN ARE ANTICIPATING INVESTMENT FROM EASTERNERS

DENVER, Sept. 20—As snow is reported in the mountains, the gold rush prepares to keep on through another Winter with the probability that there will be greater activity in the Colorado gold camps in the next few months than for many years. Gold production is expected to be 50 per cent greater here this year than in 1933, with an even bigger increase in 1935.

The latter expectation is based on the belief that when Congress convenes the gold content of the dollar will be further reduced, with a concomitant increase in price above the present $35-per-ounce level. Many mining interests claim they have assurance from Washington that the price of gold will be fixed at double the old rate of $20.67 per ounce. At such a price it would make it possible to profit from most gold-bearing ore, something of a scramble is going on to obtain options on claims that were formerly thought to be worthless, while the booming prosperity of the days of Cripple Creek is expected to return.

The more practical mining men in Denver and Colorado Springs have maintained right along that additional capital was needed before the State's gold deposits could be properly developed. . . . They point out that Eastern investors have been wary of low-grade gold properties, fearing that the gold price might be cut. This fear would be removed should the gold price be raised and fixed by mandate, which they expect Congress to do. Such action would be followed by a rush of Eastern capital seeking investment in almost anything that could be tagged as a gold mine, mining engineers feel.

Should all this actually develop, Colorado might see the end of the Depression.

Miners hoping for $60 gold were disappointed. The metal would remain at $35, but that price was more than enough for a mining boom. Between 1933 and 1934 the number of active hardrock mines as noted by the Colorado Bureau of Mines jumped from 350 to 672. Many were little more than holes in the side of a hill, where teams of two or three miners tried to make the profits that $20 gold had denied them. Nevertheless, gold production in 1936 soared to 370,000 troy ounces, the highest in fifteen years and double the output of 1930.

Placer mining understandably showed the greatest overall increase, rebounding from a mere 1,200 ounces in 1931 to 30,000 ounces by 1935, when the Colorado Bureau of Mines listed nine hundred active placer operations. They categorized only thirty as "large" operations, but those included four reactivated gold boats in Summit and Park counties. Draglining now became the most popular form of large scale, commercial placer mining. Draglining scraped overburden and gold-bearing gravels with cable-mounted buckets and steel plates into floating or dry-land washing plants, where revolving trommels, graded screens, jigs and mercury riffles efficiently recovered even fine gold particles.

Accurate estimation of placer production, meanwhile, became more difficult than ever. Historically, placer production figures, especially from small operations, were notoriously unreliable. Miners breaking even often professed to be "washing out plenty" to sell the claim at a better price. Miners washing out plenty usually said nothing.

The new federal income tax put a new light on disclosure of placer production. Small-scale placer mining was among the few professions in which the Internal Revenue Service could not generally estimate gross income. Only the miner knew what came out of his sluice, and neither the I.R.S. nor anyone else could say otherwise. The government encouraged miners to sell their raw gold and amalgam to the U.S. Mint. Many were reluctant, preferring to dispose of gold to investors, speculators, jewelers and manufacturers in receiptless transactions, selling "just enough" to the Mint to indicate a "reasonable" production. Miners, when asked about their production, often winked and offered the standard wry reply, "In God we trust," meaning that "only God and I knows what come out of these riffles, and He ain't told nobody yet and I sure ain't about to." These practices resulted in "official" placer productions figures that were probably substantially underestimated.

The renewed prospecting activity even brought a strike or two that made veteran miners remember the good old days. In June 1933 Raymond and Charles Starr were placer prospecting on Gold Run, a tributary of the East Mancos River near the town of Mancos, located in the La Plata mining district at the extreme southwest end of the Colorado Mineral Belt. Following a trail of coarse flakes, they panned their way upstream into formations of sedimentary rocks, unlikely places for lode gold to occur. Yet that was what they found—the outcrop of a quartz vein cutting right through the sandstone and shale layers, completely oxidized and carrying more than eight ounces of gold per ton. A rush followed, but the prospectors failed to find other veins. After enjoying celebrity status in the newspapers, in at least two magazines and on several radio stations, the Starr Brothers founded the Red Arrow Gold Corporation with a few local partners and began small-scale drift mining. Within five years they had recovered over 4,000 ounces of gold worth about $150,000. At a 40 percent profit, few small companies did better during the last Depression years.

Entire districts came back to life on the strength of $35 gold. Summitville, after becoming a ghost town following the 1927 Jack Pickens excitement, boomed once more. Summitville Consolidated Mines, Inc. rebuilt the decaying old camp as a company town, consolidated many properties, and by 1938 produced 30,000 ounces of gold per year. Although the Summitville ores now averaged only about a half-ounce of gold per ton, miners occasionally turned up bonanza pockets. One celebrated piece of ore mined in 1939 was immediately displayed in New York to entice potential investors. It weighed 130 pounds and contained an estimated 348 troy ounces of gold worth $12,000.

Among the economic benefits of the revaluation of gold was increased employment in Western mining districts. The London district, high in the Mosquito Range in Park County provides a good example. Since its discovery in 1875 the London vein and its associated deposits, worked by mines like the North London, South London, London Butte, London Extension, Pennsylvania and American, had yielded over 400,000 ounces of gold. By 1930 the only survivor was the American, thanks to its extraordinarily rich ore. But by 1935 the entire district had reopened, and 1,000 men found employment in six mines and the four mills that served them.

The boom in placer mining also showed that the old-timers had missed some of the big nuggets. In July 1937 the gravels of the Bulgar Placer, high on Pennsylvania Mountain in Park County, produced a beautiful nugget weighing 11.95 troy ounces—one pennyweight short of a troy pound. That gave the Bulgar Placer two major distinctions in placer mining: first, at an elevation of 12,500 feet, it was the highest production gold placer in North America. Second, the "Penn Hill nugget," the name given the 11.95-troy ounce specimen, was the largest known Colorado nugget.

Thirty-five-dollar gold also inspired construction of the South Platte Dredging Company's "Dredge No. 1," the largest floating bucketline dredge ever to operate in Colorado. The 150-foot-long steel hull drew nine feet of water; 105 thirteen-cubic-foot buckets could take down a 26-foot-high bank above the waterline or excavate to a depth of 70 feet below the waterline. At a speed of 28 buckets per minute, the dredge could gouge out and wash 15,000 cubic yards of gravel each day. A 54-foot-long grizzly and screen system "took down" gravels to 3/8 inch, dumping them into two "nugget sluices," each 33 feet long and 42 inches wide, then into 32 riffle tables, each 20 feet long and 20 inches wide. A dozen electric motors generated 2,400 horsepower, and pump capacity exceeded 21,000 gallons of water per minute. Dredge No. 1, familiarly known as the "Fairplay Dredge," began operation in 1941 on the South Platte River bottom just south of Fairplay. In its first year the big dredge washed out 9,000 ounces of gold worth about $260,000.

At Cripple Creek, $35 gold brought a 50 percent increase in gold production during the 1930s and encouraged construction of the 6½-mile, $1.25 million Carlton Tunnel to drain the entire district to a depth of 3,000 feet, paving the way for future deep mining. With most of the historic Cripple Creek properties consolidated under the Golden Cycle Corporation, completion of the Carlton Tunnel in 1941 promised dramatically increased gold production from Colorado's greatest gold district.

In 1941 Colorado produced some 380,000 troy ounces of gold worth over $13 million—the highest ounce production since 1924 and the highest dollar value since 1917. The next few years promised even further increases in production, but the gold mining boom that began with the era of $35 gold was stopped in its tracks by World War II. Immediately following the Japanese attack on Pearl Harbor, many gold miners entered military service or took higher paying jobs in the defense industry. In March 1942 mines with over one-third of the value of their output in gold or silver lost their wartime priority rating for obtaining essential materials such as steel and fuel. Gold mining had already declined when the War Production Board issued limitation order L-208, halting production of all non-essential minerals—gold and silver—to direct the full capacity of the mining industry to production of iron and the base and alloying metals.

Dredges, draglines and all large placer and primary lode gold mines shut down immediately. The board granted Cripple Creek a temporary, eight-month exemption to prepare the deep mines for shutdown and ease the economic impact on the "all-gold" district. Production was cut in half by 1943; by 1945, Colorado's annual production dropped below 100,000 ounces for the first time since 1859, and placer production was officially listed at a mere 248 ounces.

The government rescinded limitation order L-208 on July 1, 1945, weeks before the end of the war, and gold mining resumed almost immediately. Returning troops without jobs could find work in the placers; two dredges, including the big Fairplay Dredge, were reactivated, and placer production in 1946 jumped to over 20,000 ounces. Lode mines reopened more slowly, but by 1947 Colorado's annual gold production made a strong recovery to 168,000 ounces worth $5.8 million, and most believed the gold mining boom would continue right where it left off in 1941.

But 1947 was the last hurrah, for the encouraging production figures were not reflected in profits. Mine owners quickly learned that the accelerated wartime and postwar inflation rates had already caught up with $35 gold. Relative to the record costs of labor, materials and equipment, gold was as undervalued as it was in the 1920s. Gold mines that had just reopened closed in droves, and investors lost millions of dollars in capital that they had put up in the late 1930s.

111

By 1950 the nation had embarked on an unprecedented industrial boom and period of general economic prosperity, and gold miners could find good-paying jobs in any number of fields. Even the hard-core miners who wanted more drilling and blasting, as well as prospectors who sought one more chance to strike it rich, had an alternative—uranium. Trading pans and sluices for jeeps and Geiger counters, many headed for Colorado's western slope to join the West's last true mineral rush in which the individual, through discovery and claiming, still had that elusive but tantalizing chance to make a fortune.

In 1951, 90 percent of Colorado's placer production came from the South Platte Dredging Company's big Dredge No. 1. Over several years of operation, the Fairplay Dredge washed 33 million cubic yards of upper South Platte River gravels, recovering about 120,000 troy ounces, or four tons, of raw placer gold worth over $3 million. Fairplay residents were saddened to learn that 1951 would be the last year of operation for the dredge and its 24-man crew. In 1952, when the company dismantled the gold recovery system and carefully cleaned all the components, the dredge yielded its final 965 ounces of

*The South Platte Dredging Company's Dredge No. 1, familiarly known as the "Fairplay Dredge," was the biggest and the last floating bucketline dredge ever to operate in Colorado. Photo taken in 1951, the dredge's last full year of operation.* —Colorado Historical Society

gold. Surrounded by thousands of neatly stacked heaps of washed boulder tailings, the dredge remained a landmark in the flats below Fairplay, a slowly rusting symbol of the end of an era. With the shutdown of the Fairplay Dredge, Colorado's annual placer production dropped to 1,500 ounces. Most of that, for the first time, came not from gold placer mines, but as a by-product of sand and gravel-washing operations.

The only encouraging early 50s gold-mining development was the opening of Gold Cycle Gold Corporation's Carlton Mill in Cripple Creek in March 1951. The new roasting-cyanidation mill poured its first two "bricks" weighing 1,208 and 970 troy ounces, in May. Selective mining on the deeper levels of several historic mines provided ores averaging about two troy ounces of gold per ton—high grade for the 1950s.

The Carlton Mill was vital to Cripple Creek's survival as an active mining district, but had an even greater significance to the gold mining industry. When cyanidation was introduced to the United States in the 1890s, zinc precipitation provided the only method of recovering the dissolved gold from the weak, pregnant cyanide solutions. But as ore grades declined and the cost of zinc rose, metallurgists began studying other methods, especially carbon adsorption. The ability of activated carbon particles to attract, or adsorb, gold from solution had been patented as a potential extraction process in 1894. But metallurgists still needed a way to cheaply and quickly "desorb" the gold from the carbon. In the only known extraction operation, the gold was separated by flotation then smelted to burn off the remaining carbon, a process just as slow and expensive as zinc precipitation.

In 1951 Golden Cycle Gold Corporation metallurgists along with researchers from the United States Bureau of Mines designed and tested the first commercial carbon adsorption-desorption process in "a corner" of the Carlton Mill. They first concentrated the low-grade telluride ores by flotation, roasted them to drive off the tellurium, and treated them with dilute sodium cyanide solution to dissolve the gold. They then agitated the pregnant cyanide solution with granules of activated charcoal made from charred apricot and peach pits, a durable form of charcoal. The new desorption process began when the "loaded" charcoal went into a heat-pressure vessel where ammonia redissolved, or "stripped," the gold, forming a very concentrated, gold-rich stripper solution. From this solution a small amount of zinc quickly precipitated the gold as a metallic sludge. The process eliminated carbon flotation and smelting, and, allowed mill operators to recycle both the carbon granules and reagents.

While metallurgically brilliant, the delicate process functioned poorly in the rough environment of mills not specifically designed for it, including the Carlton. Although years ahead of its time, the Carlton Mill pioneered the carbon desorption process, that, in time, was adopted in gold mining worldwide.

Although miners and mill operators wrestled with the problems of lower-grade ores, Cripple Creek occasionally provided some of the old excitement of the boom days. In August 1953 miners in the Ajax drilled into two vugs lined with crystals of calaverite and sylvanite. In September *The Engineering and Mining Journal* reported:

> Cripple Creek is buzzing with excitement as word spread that two "Aladdin's caves of gold" have been discovered on the 31st or bottom 3100-foot-level of the Ajax Mine on Battle Mountain. Not since 1914 when the famed $1,200,000 vug was found on the 12th level of the Cresson Mine, has ore of such Croesus-like richness been reported. Officials of the Golden Cycle Corp., owner of the mine, estimate the ore may be worth as much as $40 to $50 dollars per pound (up to 2,500 troy ounces per ton). The two underground vaults were blasted into recently. The walls of the highly mineralized caves glistened with sylvanite and calaverite. "It is a sight a mining man may see but once in a lifetime it he's lucky," was the feeling expressed by M. H. Grice, superintendent of the mine, when he first viewed the bonanza.

But the Cripple Creek vugs only offered a brief diversion, and the Colorado gold mining industry, burdened by lower ore grades, higher operating costs and the fixed price of its product, continued steadily downhill. By 1960 Colorado's annual gold production sagged to 66,000 ounces. In 1967 it hit rock bottom with only 22,000 ounces, the lowest since 1859.

By then the United States, including Alaska, had produced an estimated 307 million troy ounces—about 10,000 standard tons—of gold. In nearly 110 years of organized mining, Colorado accounted for 13.3 percent of it with an estimated official production of 41 million troy ounces—over 1,400 standard tons—worth about one billion dollars, ranking second among the states only to California. Lode mines produced about 98 percent of Colorado's gold, with half of that coming from Cripple Creek. Among all United States gold-producing districts, only Lead, South Dakota, site of the great Homestake Mine, surpassed Cripple Creek's cumulative production up to 1967.

The search for Colorado's gold had led prospectors to enormous deposits of silver, lead, zinc, copper and molybdenum. Nevertheless, for well over a century gold remained the state's most valuable mineral product; in 1967, gold was displaced by molybdenum.

A gold prospector, Charles Senter, discovered the great Climax molybdenum deposit in 1879. Trying to find the lode source of the gold in McNulty Gulch, one of the Summit County "pound diggings" of the 1860s, Senter instead found an unknown type of mineralization high on Bartlett Mountain above Fremont Pass. Assuming, or perhaps hoping, it contained gold, he named his claims the Gold Reef series. Almost twenty years later, mineralogists learned that Senter's mineralization was molybdenum disulfide, and molybdenum mining finally began in 1917. In 1967 the Climax Molybdenum Company was the largest underground mine in the world, and the value of its "gray gold" surpassed that of all the gold mined in Colorado. In another development symbolic of the decline of gold mining in Colorado, the enormous Climax tailings pond began to slowly cover the old pound diggings of McNulty Gulch.

As the 1960s drew to an end, the story of Colorado gold and the mines that produced it seemed consigned to the history books.

*Do you want to see some gold? Jump in my truck and I'll show you—it's going to take two of us anyway to put it in my pickup.*

—Bob Ellithorpe to Chuck Beverly,
ASARCO geologist at Summitville, October 3, 1975

# 7

# FREE MARKET GOLD: RESTORING THE GLITTER
## 1970 – the present

Gold miners were the first to be adversely affected by the increasing undervaluation of $35 gold. By the mid-1960s, however, the U.S. Treasury felt the effects. As the spot price of gold drifted above $35 per troy ounce on international markets, the Treasury dumped huge amounts of gold bullion reserves on the open market in a determined effort to "hold the line" on $35 gold. Weak world mine supply fell far short of record demand for gold. Many new applications in the aerospace and electronics industries used gold, and, as the Vietnam War intensified many foreign investors hurriedly converted assets and paper currencies into gold.

Speculation in gold soared in 1968 when Great Britain devalued its pound sterling against gold, and an awkward, two-tiered pricing system emerged in international markets. Most central banks traded gold at the fixed $35 price, while brokers employed a fluctuating price based partially on supply and demand. By 1972 "free" gold reached $70 per ounce and most governments abandoned their efforts to hold the line on $35 gold. The following year the U. S. Treasury formally devalued the dollar, boosting the "free" price to $90. Finally, on December 31, 1974, the Treasury lifted all restrictions on gold, legalizing ownership and trading of the metal in all forms for the first time since 1933. As a free market commodity with its price deter-

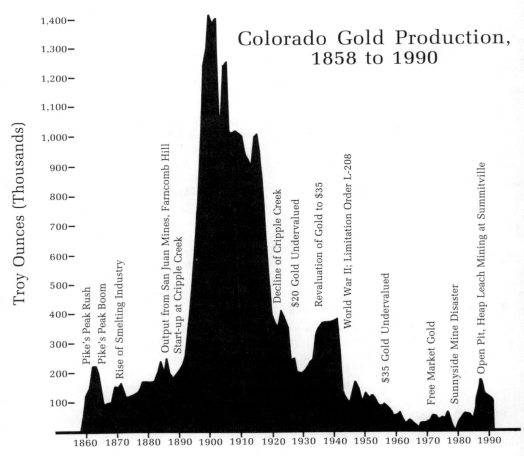

Colorado Gold Production, 1858 to 1990

Troy Ounces (Thousands)

1,400—
1,300—
1,200—
1,100—
1,000—
900—
800—
700—
600—
500—
400—
300—
200—
100—

1860  1870  1880  1890  1900  1910  1920  1930  1940  1950  1960  1970  1980  1990

Years

Pike's Peak Rush
Pike's Peak Boom
Rise of Smelting Industry
Output from San Juan Mines, Farncomb Hill
Start-up at Cripple Creek
Decline of Cripple Creek
$20 Gold Undervalued
Revaluation of Gold to $35
World War II; Limitation Order L-208
$35 Gold Undervalued
Free Market Gold
Sunnyside Mine Disaster
Open Pit, Heap Leach Mining at Summitville

118

mined solely by supply and demand, gold soon topped $200 on the way to its 1980 historic high of just over $800 per troy ounce.

The effects of free-market gold in Colorado were unlike those that followed the revaluation of gold in 1933. Then, many experienced gold miners eagerly returned to the placers and lode deposits, often going back to the one profession they knew and, also, often to the only job they could get. But by the 1970s Colorado had few experienced gold miners left, and most of them had other jobs with good wages and security.

While Colorado saw no immediate rush to pick-and-shovel mining, many people chose to associate themselves with gold mining vicariously, mainly through speculation and investment. By 1978 when gold topped $350 per troy ounce, investors found the potential profits from gold-related investments were hard to ignore. Placer gravels grading 20 cents per cubic yard in 1972 were suddenly worth $2 per cubic yard. A ton of ore carrying a half-ounce of gold was no longer worth $17.50, but $175. Even those old low-grade mine wastes and mill tailings, of which Colorado had plenty, looked, at least on paper, like sure-fire bonanza investments—and promoters knew it.

"A gold mine," Mark Twain once commented, "is a hole in the ground with a liar at the top," words that rang true in the 1970s. The Colorado Attorney General's Office began receiving complaints from investors who had bought into "a Colorado gold mine" by handing a check, as it turned out, to "a liar at the top." With the historic association of the words "Colorado" and "gold," promoters and swindlers had a field day, especially in the Florida retirement communities where wealthy retirees from the Northeast, as one promoter put it, "didn't know a mine from a pine."

Scams seemed limitless in their variety. Promoters took potential investors who actually visited Colorado on mine site tours then presented them with samples—usually salted—and the inflated assay reports that "confirmed" them. "Dirt pile" scams enjoyed great success, especially when they were located near a well-known district like Cripple Creek or Central City. Promoters gave investors the opportunity to purchase "dirt" containing a purported "ounce a ton," at "below spot market prices," in lots of as few as ten tons or, for those who wanted to get rich quick, thousands of tons. Investors believed they were buying "gold in the ground," and that's exactly where it stayed, for the purchase agreements lacked provisions for technicalities such as mining, milling, transporting and extracting.

The 1970s also saw more gold claims staked in Colorado than at any time since the 1930s, most for pure speculation. Placer claims near places like Breckenridge and Fairplay, "where they took out millions during the rush," sold like hotcakes. Gullible investors could either "hold 'em for the future" or, as they were told with a wink, "get out there and mine 'em yourself." Few, however, contained economic grades of gravel, and many were located in areas where new environmental and zoning regulations prohibited mining.

The most popular of all the gold mine scams was "dump leaching," a term that in the 1970s had almost magical connotations. Dump-leach projects relied on cyanidation, a process few potential investors understood yet accepted as a dirt-cheap, foolproof way to squeeze gold out of rock. For proof of what cyanidation could do, promoters had only to point at Nevada's Carlin Mine, which since 1962 had revolutionized the gold-mining industry. The Carlin, using mass open-pit mining, simple crushing, and cyanidation extraction in huge leach pads, was making a healthy profit on ores grading only 0.06 ounces of gold per ton.

Investors jumped at the opportunity to buy into dump-leach projects that either already owned or would purchase for next to nothing old mine wastes and mill tailings containing more gold per ton than the Carlin ores. The projects would blade the material into a holding pad, leach it with cyanide, and divide the profits among the investors. Although dump leaching seemed a sure thing on paper, most investors lost everything. Few of the operators who actually tried it understood the complex chemistry and the limitations of cyanidation, much less the expense and mechanics of recovering dissolved gold from the pregnant solutions. Unfortunately, most failed to see the necessity of well-designed, impervious leach pads. Several poorly constructed pads leaked cyanide, resulting in environmental mini-disasters.

Following the revaluation of gold in 1933, Colorado had hundreds of placer-mining operations, but in the late 1970s only one commercial, primary placer mine operated in the entire state. Located at the foot of Mt. Elbert in Lake County, the placer had been discovered, staked and developed by a "mom and pop" team of miners, Fred and Eileen Garner of Leadville. Fred Garner got his start in placer mining in 1932 at age twenty, when C. V. Hallenbeck, one of Colorado's last big placer developers, hired him to run a power shovel on the dragline operation on Box Creek.

Box Creek had already produced 50,000 ounces of gold but had plenty left, mostly in deep pay streaks near bedrock—a dense impermeable clay with an undulating irregular surface. "It was a lot of work to go through twenty feet or more of overburden," Garner recalled, "but when that dirt went into the sluices, there was so much gold in the top riffles there wasn't room for the black sand."

120

Garner remembered a rare "glory hole," a small bedrock depression that had been a near-perfect trap for the alluvial gold. "It was about seven feet long and three feet deep, too small to work with the dragline," he said. "We put a smooth scraper edge on a loader bucket and cleaned it out ourselves. You could actually see the gold coming up in the bucket. Gold was only thirty-five then, and Hallenbeck got about fifty thousand dollars out of that one hole, enough to buy him two new Packards and a ranch."

When limitation order L-208 halted gold mining in 1942, Garner became an operating engineer in the army "for the duration." The draglining operation in Box Creek lasted only a few more years after the war, then shut down permanently. Now married, Garner worked a variety of construction jobs. On his days off, he and Eileen would "walk the hills," prospecting for gold. In summer 1953 they investigated an area above Box Creek that had never been mined before. A heavy rain had washed out some gullies, and Garner noticed pieces of epidote, a relatively heavy green mineral common in the Box Creek pay streaks. "I took some pans right off the top," Garner said. "When I saw forty, fifty, even eighty colors to the pan, I knew right then what we had."

They located and filed claims on the U.S. Forest Service land but didn't rush into mining. Garner continued working different jobs, sometimes taking his pay in the use of an eight-inch core drill. At the rate of only one hole per season, Garner eventually drilled and sampled eleven 20-foot-deep holes that revealed the horizontal and vertical configuration of the placer, including bedrock gravels running as high as $7.50 per cubic yard. He also picked up the equipment he'd need, mostly at auction from other placer operations that were going broke all over the state.

When they finally began mining in 1966, the Garners lived in a small trailer on the claims and trucked the gravel to their washing plant a mile away. They recovered the coarse gold, including "nuggets as big as the end of my thumb," by washing, the fine gold by almagamation. "When we needed cash, we'd sell the amalgam to the Denver Mint," Garner remembered. "They'd give us a receipt for anything over two ounces. After they tested and retorted it, we'd get a Treasury Department check a week or two later. But the coarse gold went into a bank deposit box. That was our retirement."

Commercial placer mines were rare in the 1970s, and, as the soaring price of gold restored the metal's intrigue, problems with the public became inevitable at the Garner's operation. Although the isolated, secluded mine property was well-posted against trespassing, the Garners had all-too-frequent unannounced visits by amateur gold panners, prowlers and the curious. "I guess they thought the gold was just layin' all over the top of the ground," Garner said. "I'd throw 'em off, but there would always be more."

In 1975 an armed intruder refused to leave the property. That resulted in an argument over a rifle, a knife fight, involvement of sheriff's deputies, and minor hospitalization for both Garner and his assailant. A few months later the Garners awoke to gunshots in the night. Investigating, Garner found four rustlers shooting and quartering the cattle that roamed across the claims. After a brief gunfight, Garner apprehended all four. Ultimately, however, the "Wild West" episodes improved mine security. "After that deal with the rustlers hit the papers," Garner recalled, "you couldn't find anybody within a mile of those claims."

Garner's biggest fight was with the United States government. The Garners' claims were located near a major water diversion project involving the U. S. Forest Service, the Bureau of Reclamation and the Bureau of Land Management, which jointly announced their intent to appropriate the claims in return for "fair" payment." "But there was nothing fair about it," Garner complained. "Those claims weren't just some undeveloped rural land. They were a profitable gold mine, our living and our retirement—everything we had worked for. We spent money on lawyers, but the government just gave us the run-around like we didn't matter. I never scared easy, but trying to fight the government scared me."

In desperation the Garners finally sought help at the Rocky Mountain Legal Foundation offices in Denver, meeting a "young lawyer" who sympathized with them but wasn't in a position to help. In 1982 they were about to lose the claims; with no one else to turn to, they decided to track down the young lawyer they met in Denver years before. They found him in Washington, where the lawyer— James Watt—had just been appointed United States Secretary of the Interior. "He remembered us," Garner said. "I never knew exactly what he did, but all of a sudden those government people who would never give me five minutes of their time are calling me for an appointment at my convenience. Seems they didn't need our claims after all. After that, we got our price, sold out and retired. All in all, I'd have to say gold treated us pretty good."

Even with the record gold prices, few other commercial placer miners could say the same, for estimated placer production amounted to only a few hundred ounces per year. In 1980 the biggest and most familiar symbol of Colorado's placer mining history, the "Fairplay Dredge," which had stood as a monument in the tailing heaps south of Fairplay, was dismantled and shipped to South America.

The era of high-priced, free-market gold failed to bring the boom in lode-gold mining that the revaluation of gold in 1933 did. Many mining companies were cautious about jumping back into gold in the 1970s for two reasons: First, speculation still largely determined the price of gold, and it had yet to stabilize at a level that reflected true supply and demand. Second, and equally important, the companies were concerned about the costs of complying with strict new environmental regulations that now affected all mining operations. Nevertheless, Colorado's annual gold production doubled from only 37,000 ounces in 1972 to 72,000 ounces by 1978. About half of the 1970s gold production came from a single mine—the Sunnyside. High above Silverton in San Juan County, the Sunnyside was a classic example of an old mine that was far from "played out."

Prospectors discovered the original Sunny Side vein in a lightning storm in the summer of 1873. Cumulative production topped one million ounces of gold by 1929, when the Sunnyside Mine fell victim to the stock market crash and was mothballed. The 1930s saw limited development work, and the mine remained largely inactive after World War II.

In 1959 Standard Metals Corporation acquired the property and extended the old American Tunnel into the lower mineralized zones of the Sunnyside vein. They produced lead-zinc on a break-even basis until they encountered some rich gold mineralization in 1969. Believing the gold to be just another small erratic pocket, management mined the immediate reserves, then shut the mine down. Three years later the company had the property surveyed again; this time, modern electromagnetic methods revealed large mineralized anomalies. The first drill cores taken in 1973—a century after the vein had been discovered—showed high grades of lead, silver, zinc and copper, and gold so rich that wires of native metal were visible in the core sections. The new vein shoot, named the Little Mary, became one of the richest ever found in the San Juans. It yielded 30,000 ounces of gold for each of the next five years.

Like many other big San Juan mines at or above timberline, the Sunnyside survived avalanches and fires during its long life. In 1978, at the peak of production, disaster again struck the Sunnyside—one of the most bizarre accidents in American mining history. Mining had reached an upper stope on the Spur vein, directly beneath 12,300-foot-high Lake Emma. The top of the stope was only 70 feet below the bed of the alpine lake, and core drilling had indicated the overhead rock safe. But it wasn't, and on June 4th Lake Emma burst through with a raging torrent of water and a million tons of mud that fell 1,800 vertical feet through the Sunnyside workings, tearing out timbers and pipes, and completely filling the two-mile-long American Tunnel with mud and debris. The disaster occurred on a Sunday, when the mine's 125 men were off work. Had it happened a day later, everyone underground would have perished. A 65-foot-long, 20-foot-diameter "sliver" of the vein had apparently been scoured out by Pleistocene glaciers, leaving a gap in the otherwise solid rock that the core drills had missed, and a space for the water and mud to burst through.

Without the Sunnyside, Colorado's 1979 gold production plummeted to 13,800 ounces, an all-time low. Nearly three-quarters of the 1979 total came from ASARCO's Black Cloud Mine at Leadville, a

*Headframe of the Black Cloud Mine at Leadville, Colorado. Owned and operated by the ASARCO-Resurrection Joint Venture, the Black Cloud has produced lead, zinc, silver and 10,000 ounces of gold each year since 1975.*

*Tom Hendricks (center) reopened the Cross Mine as a one-man pick-and-shovel operation. Today, the Cross is an important gold producer with large reserves.* —courtesy Hendricks Mining Company

steady producer of lead-zinc-silver-gold since 1974. After eighteen months of restoration, the Sunnyside resumed production in 1980, raising Colorado's annual gold output to 39,400 ounces.

Colorado once had hundreds of small lode gold mines. But declining ore grades, depressed metal markets and, since 1980, the high costs of complying with new environmental, health and safety regulations, had made life increasingly difficult for small hardrock-mining operations. The best known of the few successful small-scale hardrock gold miners is Thomas S. Hendricks, whose reactivation of Cross Mine, high in the Caribou district in western Boulder Country, has received national attention.

The Cross vein was discovered in 1873, worked intermittently, and developed to its fourth level before being shut down in World War II. Not much happened at the Cross until 1974 when Hendricks, fresh out of high school, leased the property under the name of the Hendricks Mining Company. While studying geology in his spare time, he dewatered the mine and reopened it as a one-man pick-and-shovel operation. He then undertook a simultaneous exploration and development program, using the income from limited mining to cover his expenses while he determined what the Cross had left. As he

125

suspected, the Cross had a great deal left; by 1983; Hendricks had shipped 5,000 ounces of gold along with quantities of silver, lead, zinc and copper. He found the results of an extensive core-drilling program he started in 1981 much more important. Seventy-one holes, totaling 28,800 feet of drilling, revealed forty-four mineralized veins and small stockwork ore bodies. Hendricks used the core data to generate three-dimensional computer pictures that geologically interpreted most of the complex deposit. He has pegged reserves in the Cross at 130,000 ounces of gold, much of it in ore amenable to selective mining and grading 0.364 ounces per ton—high by today's standards. Hendricks and his mining accomplishments have been featured in *Newsweek*, major mining trade journals and Denver-area newspapers, and on all Denver television affiliates. He has also emerged as a leading spokesman for all miners in Colorado, and his mine tours and speaking engagements have enhanced the overall public image of mining.

The Sunnyside and the Cross weren't the only gold mines in the 1970s and 1980s to show they had gold remaining; the biggest surprise came out of Summitville, the 11,300-foot-high camp in the San Juan Mountains of Rio Grande County. Summitville went through so many booms and busts that even the old-timers had lost count. After the revival of the 1930s, Summitville shut down during World War II, then managed a brief comeback in 1947. By then, the Summitville district had produced some 270,000 ounces of gold worth nearly $8 million. All of it had been extracted from only 300,000 tons of ore—a seventy-five-year grade average of almost one troy ounce per ton. But Summitville closed again in 1949, many thought for the last time.

Exploration geologists returned to Summitville in 1965 looking for copper, not gold. By the 1970s, however, when gold began its historic price rise, geologists were looking for both metals. ASARCO, Inc., had leased many properties from the Reynolds Mining Company and their exploration proceeded quietly until Bob Ellithorpe, an independent subcontractor, made a remarkable discovery. Although Ellithorpe was contracting as an equipment operator, he was also a prospector. Geologist Mark Coolbaugh, writing in *The San Luis Valley Historian*, later noted that what Bob Ellithorpe knew about gold, he had learned from some of the best:

> The Ellithorpe family had a long history of prospecting and mining in the area. The father, Harry Ellithorpe, had worked for Jack Pickens in the twenties assaying his ore. It was said Harry Ellithorpe could break a rock, pan it, and give an assay on it by the string in the pan—like a cook so used to measuring he didn't

need a cup or spoon. He had raised his sons in proper prospecting fashion: when he took them hunting and fishing it was for rocks and minerals, up timbered mountainsides and down old mine shafts. Because of this, Bob Ellithorpe, the youngest son, had developed on uncanny instinct for ore—he was able to see things others missed.

In the late afternoon of October 3, 1975, Ellithorpe had finished some grading and parked his bulldozer just north of the portal of the old Dexter Mine. What happened next has been retold many times in many versions. The following account, however, comes from the official report of Chuck Beverly, ASARCO's geologist-in-charge at Summitville:

> While Bob Ellithorpe was climbing back up on his dozer, he noticed a large piece of float in the roadcut that "had a yellow streak in it." He later told me that he did not examine it closely at the time but kept thinking about it and after work that day about 5:00 p.m. when he took Bob back up the hill to retrieve his pickup truck he proceeded down on a different route to the boarding house and stopped to examine the "yellow streak" more closely. Up to this point no one but Bob Ellithorpe knew anything about the gold-bearing rock.
>
> About 5:30 p.m. that day, I was refueling my Blazer when Bob suddenly drove up and jumped out of his pickup truck. I immediately, jokingly, said, "Do you want me to fill yours up too?" He looked at me quite seriously and said, "No—do you want to see some gold?", to which I replied, "Sure." Bob Ellithorpe then stated, "At least I think it's gold—if I show you where it is, will you promise to give me half of it?, and I replied, "Sure." Bob then said, "Jump in my truck and I'll show you—it's going to take two of us anyway to put in my pickup." At this point I started to laugh and said, "Oh sure it will, Bob." The reason for this was that all summer long Bob, as well as other ASARCO employees, had brought me "specimens" they had found, some bearing gold and some not, but up until this time no gold had been found that was larger than a pinhead in size.
>
> It took about ten minutes to drive to the placer where Bob found the gold. During this time, I questioned him further about it, asking him how big it was and if it was float or in place. He came directly to me, I think, because of the mutual trust we had built up over the course of the summer, and he had not moved the rock. When he stopped the truck and I stepped out, the "yellow streak" was obvious from four feet away. I examined it further with a hand lens and verified that it was indeed gold and stated that "the large rock had more gold in it than I had ever seen." I said, "It was bigger than anything in the Denver Museum." Bob

agreed We decided to show the specimen to other workers on the project; but, since the sun had set, we'd leave it in place until the morning sun shone on it and we could document it in place with photos . . .

The float boulder (18 inches x approximately 12 inches in diameter and weighing 141.5 pounds) is intrusive breccia consisting of silicified vuggy quartz latite fragments cemented with a matrix of very fine-grained crystalline quartz, barite and gold. The gold appears to wrap around most of the fragments in a spectacular arrangement. The largest gold vein measures 12 inches by 0.6 inches and appears to cut entirely through the breccia mass.

Beverly and Ellithorpe guessed that the rock had broken off a high outcrop in the area of the original Little Annie vein, then moved downhill by natural processes to the point where Ellithorp found it. It had probably been completely covered in the 1930s; otherwise it would almost certainly have been discovered during that decade's intensive mining activity. However, the rock appeared to have been fully exposed by the side of a public road for at least the last ten years waiting for someone to find it.

Exactly what to do with the "Summitville gold boulder," as the specimen became known, presented ASARCO with a problem. When Beverly reported the discovery to the ASARCO offices in Denver, he explained the "fifty-fifty" agreement he had made verbally with Ellithorpe. Traditionally, prospectors providing a company with mineral location information received a ten percent finder's fee—if investigation proved the find was worth claiming. But Ellithorpe discovered not an in-place deposit, but a piece of alluvial float. Another question concerned Chuck Beverly's legal right to negotiate on behalf of the company.

Meanwhile, Bob Ellithorpe's father, Harry, then in his eighties and dying of cancer in Colorado Springs, was able to make one last trip to Summitville. Posing for photographs with his son and the Summitville gold boulder, the old prospector commented, "That's the kind of thing we found in the old days. Maybe even better." Harry Ellithorpe lived only one more month, but he enjoyed the satisfaction of knowing his son had made the big find that had eluded him in his younger days.

When ASARCO had accurately determined the volume, normal weight and specific gravity of the gold boulder, they estimated the contained gold at 350 troy ounces. With gold then worth $150 per troy ounce, they calculated the bullion value of the boulder at just over $50,000. But as a rare and spectacular specimen, the boulder was

*Harry Ellithorpe (left) and his son Bob examine the Summitville Gold Boulder at Summitville shortly after its discovery in October 1975.*
—Ron Pochon

worth several times that amount. ASARCO settled the question of finder's fee by offering Bob Ellithorpe $21,000, which he accepted.

In order to avert a "gold rush," ASARCO kept the discovery a secret for over a year, finally announcing it in late fall 1976, just as Summitville was about to be snowed in for the winter. With the agreement of the landowner, the Reynolds Mining Company, ASARCO donated the Summitville gold boulder to the Denver Museum of Natural History. By then, because of higher gold prices and a greater appreciation of the rarity of the celebrated boulder, its specimen value had increased considerably, as noted in *The Denver Post* on November 25, 1976:

PROSPECTOR'S FIRST GOLD "SPECK"
IS 141 POUNDS—STATE'S BIGGEST

... What Ellithorpe found was a 141-pound gold rock—the largest ever found in Colorado. . . .

At the time, Ellithorpe who was doing some subcontracting work for ASARCO, couldn't believe this luck. In fact, he didn't believe it.

"I've learned over the years to leave myself an out," the gold prospector said. "I didn't want the streak to be a streak of yellow iron or fool's gold."

. . . Beverly remembers how he, Ellithorpe and others sat around figuring what it might be worth—maybe $500 to $8,000. But when it was finally analyzed, the rock's value was set at more like $350,000.

Ellithorpe and Beverly said it never entered their minds to keep the secret to themselves.

"I could have stolen the rock," Ellithorpe said. "But it really didn't enter my mind. I don't think we realized the magnitude of our find."

"Basically, we're honest people," Beverly added. "When you find something like this, it overwhelms you. I'm happy the gold is going to where Bob and I wanted it to go. Both of us felt it belonged in a museum and that it belonged in a Denver museum because it was a Colorado rock."

. . . Beverly estimates the boulder had been exposed and waiting for discovery for more than thirty years.

"During that time I would hate to say what number of people drove by it, including all those geologists," he said laughing.

Ellithorpe said he found the boulder only a few hundred yards from property he owns. And sure, he said, he had "second thoughts" about why he didn't move the stone onto his own land. But the prospector added, smiling, "We were awarded a substantial finder's fee."

As expected, the first of the treasure hunters and gold prospectors arrived in Summitville in April 1977 on snowmobiles, before the roads were even passable for vehicles. They came with everything from gold pans and picks and shovels to divining rods and metal detectors. By June, some were getting in the way of exploration work and ASARCO, concerned about safety, closed off a few of the roads. It is unlikely anyone found another gold boulder; if anyone did, they never reported it.

Although the Summitville gold boulder captured the headlines, the more significant discovery was low-grade gold mineralization extending outward from the original, mined-out high-grade veins. The lease passed from ASARCO to Anaconda Minerals in 1979, then on to Galactic Resources, Ltd., a Canadian resource development company. Galactic established the Summitville Consolidated Mining Company, completed the drilling program already underway, delineating a 25-million-ton deposit grading only 0.46 ounces of gold per ton, and announced plans to develop it with modern open-pit heap-leach methods. When they began construction of the mine and mill late in 1985, the work force of four hundred had to be bussed over eighteen miles of snow-covered mountain roads from the town of South Fork. Avalanches delayed progress, but Summitville, the highest open-pit heap-leach gold mine in the world, began production in May 1986.

Summitville mined its ore from open bench cuts in the north face of South Mountain, at elevations ranging from 11,400 feet to nearly the summit of 12,300 feet. They drilled and blasted about 29,000 tons of ore per day, transporting it by big diesel-electric trucks then crushing it. The mine produced two types of ores; the mill added lime to the silica ore, and pelletized the clay ore with cement to assure the materials were permeable in the leach pad. Lime and cement also created an alkaline environment within the heap, increasing the efficiency of the cyanidation and preventing hydrogen cyanide gas from forming. The base of its huge, bowl-like leach pad was constructed of thick layers of high-density, polyethylene liner and a reinforced, tough geotextile fabric, all sandwiched between two-foot-thick layers of compacted clay, making a self-contained system. The Summitville pad covered 137 acres (about a quarter square mile) and was eventually filled with crushed, treated ore to a depth of 400 feet.

A movable pipe system sprayed a dilute, alkaline sodium cyanide solution over the surface of the heaped ore. The solution slowly percolated downward, dissolving the gold and silver, and accumulating in a sump from which it was pumped to the surface. The pregnant cyanide solution, containing only 0.025 ounces of gold-silver per ton (about 220 gallons) then passed through a six-stage, countercurrent carbon adsorption module at the rate of 3,000 gallons per minute. Each ton of activated charcoal, prepared from charred coconut shell, adsorbed about 200 ounces of metals from solution. The loaded carbon then went to a pressurized stripper circuit, where a hot, caustic cyanide solution redissolved the gold-silver into a concentrated, pregnant stripper solution containing 12 ounces of metal per ton.

Zinc dust precipitated the gold-silver out of the stripper solution as a metallic sludge, which was mixed with diatomaceous earth and collected as a wet "cake" in a filter press. An electric furnace melted the cake, recovering the gold-silver as buttons of doré, a gold-silver

*The modern operation of the Summitville Consolidated Mining Company as seen from the top of South Mountain.*

*Ruins of the old company town buildings at Summitville as they appeared in the late 1980s. They are very near the workings of the modern open pit mine.*

alloy. The doré buttons were remelted and poured into bars containing 85 percent gold. At peak production, Summitville poured a 900-troy ounce doré bar every three days, and became Colorado's largest gold mine. Even though the high elevation limited mining to a six-month season, by the end of 1990 the Summitville Consolidated Mining Company had produced 271,000 troy ounces—nearly nine standard tons—of gold, exceeding in just five years the amount of gold produced by the old Summitville mines over an entire century.

By the mid-1980s activity had picked up in many old gold districts. At Central City, Saratoga Mines, Inc., began processing 80,000 tons of tailings from the old Saratoga No. 1 and No. 2 mines, some of which dated back to 1859. Four companies were active at Cripple Creek—Golden Cycle Gold Corp., Silver State Mining Corp., Cripple Creek and Victor Gold Mining Co., and Gold Ore, Ltd.—evaluating tailings and low-grade ores, and even considering reopening historic producers like the Ajax and Cresson Mines. The London Mines shipped limited gold and silver concentrates for the first time since World War II, while the Camp Bird shipped selected ores that, at 0.5 ounces per ton, were among the highest grade still mined in Colorado. By 1987 Colorado's gold output from fourteen active mines and leach projects topped 188,000 ounces worth about $65 million—the highest ounce production since 1941.

While no one returned to work the old Cherry Creek gravels, Denver enjoyed a gold rush of its own, corporate style. By 1988 thirty-six state, national and international gold-mining companies had established headquarters or major regional offices in Denver, taking advantage of the central location of its numerous western assay offices and mining-related businesses, and the nearby facilities of the Colorado School of Mines, U. S. Bureau of Mines and U. S. Geological Survey. Denver-based companies mined half of the record 1990 U. S. gold production of 9.9 million troy ounces.

Just as the Summitville mine neared the end of its planned six-year life, Colorado's newest gold mine came on line. Battle Mountain Gold Company's San Luis Project, located just east of San Luis in Costilla County, began open-pit mining on a 12 million-ton ore body grading 0.04 ounces of gold per ton. The San Luis Project extracts its gold by cyanidation vat leaching and recovers it by electrowinning, a method that electro-plates the gold out of the caustic stripper solution onto a sponge resembling steel wool. The project smelts the gold-laden sponge in an electric furnace, slags it, and pours it into doré bars. The company estimates reserves at 490,000 ounces of gold and mine life, figured at a production rate of 50,000 ounces of gold per year, at seven to ten years.

While most of Colorado's gold production now comes from a few large mines, the smallest mines can still make headlines. Only two primary placer gold mines were active in 1990, but one produced the second largest Colorado nugget know to exist. Like the Summitville gold boulder, the "turtle nugget" went where many thought it belongs—the Denver Museum of Natural History, as reported by *The Denver Post* on October 19, 1990:

### COLORADO WILL KEEP PRIZE
### MUSEUM IN DENVER BUYS LARGE NUGGET

... The nugget is valued at over $31,000, measures 3 inches by 1 1/2 long ("huge by Colorado standards," according to geology curator Jack Murphy), and weighs in at 8 troy ounces or 8.6 standard ounces.

The museum just acquired the piece from Colorado miner Joe Dodge, who wanted it to remain in the state rather than end up in a private, faraway collection.

Dodge's son, Shane, spotted the nugget last August in alluvial gravel at the family's Pennsylvania Mountain mine, a surface operation 12,000 feet up and about 4 miles west of Alma.

*Colorado's newest gold mine, the San Luis Project, went into production in 1991 in Costilla County. Here, the extraction plant is nearing completion.*
—courtesy Battle Mountain Gold Company

Dodge sold the "turtle nugget," named for its shape, at an undisclosed price to the museum rather than opening up a competitive bidding process.

... "I've been in Colorado mining for 37 years and felt a sense of responsibility that this nugget should remain in Colorado rather than ending up in Texas or Japan," Dodge said.

When Shane Dodge spotted the turtle nugget high on the side of Pennsylvania Mountain in August 1990, the price of gold was $380. The bullion value of the nugget was, therefore, approximately $2,600. But, just as with the Summitville gold boulder, the rarity and historical significance of the nugget added to its value. As a museum specimen, the turtle nugget became worth about $3,800 per ounce.

*. . ."placer mining" . . . is the most fascinating pursuit in the world.*

—Ovando J. Hollister, *The Mines of Colorado,* 1867

*Once gold hit six hundred dollars, we couldn't keep pans in stock or make dredges fast enough.*

Gary Christopher, proprietor,
The Prospector's Cache, Englewood, CO, 1991

# 8

# Recreational Mining: The Popular Romance

Today, summer travelers passing through Colorado's gold country find a surprising amount of gold mining activity. The same creeks and gulches once worked by the '59ers are still worked, not commercially by professional miners but by growing numbers of men, women and children, even by whole families and clubs. These amateur prospectors come equipped with gold pans, shovels and sluices, as well as concentrating wheels, metal detectors and other sophisticated gadgets at which the '59ers would only shake their heads. Few of these modern-day placer miners need the gold they find, at least in the financial sense. Instead, they want what gold mining represents: the challenge and the adventure and the thrill of the largely imaginary chance to strike it rich—all a part of the enduring romance associated with the search for gold. Recreational gold mining is a relatively recent phenomenon that participants often see as a sport or a hobby, a form of outdoor recreation similar to hunting, fishing or hiking. It's a prime example of how the American perception of gold mining has changed.

Americans have always associated gold mining with striking it rich. Yet only during the Pike's Peak rush and in the years immediately following it, did the individual have a realistic—however slim—chance of doing that. For every George Jackson and John Gregory, thousands of others prospectors trekked up the wrong gulch or arrived too late at the right gulch. After the great gulch strikes, placer mining quickly settled into a mundane commercial business of washing always more gravel to recover always less gold. Although with occasional, celebrated exceptions, placer miners learned to be satisfied with washing out a living, not a fortune.

Lode-gold prospecting was little different in Colorado. A few prospectors made fabulous strikes high in the San Juans, at Farncomb Hill, and at Cripple Creek. But for every Thomas Walsh who struck it rich, many thousands of hardrock prospectors had their own Camp Birds elude them. Most of the men who mined Colorado's gold experienced little romance and adventure. Instead, placer mining meant hands and feet numbed by icy water and backs wearied by the picks and shovels. Lode-gold mining meant long shifts of darkness and danger, with dynamite fumes and thundering drills and clouds of rock dust—all for three or four dollars per shift and, for lucky miners, a little high-grade on the side.

In the 1950s many Coloradans had firsthand knowledge of gold mining from long underground shifts, washing out a dollar a day during the Depression, the never ending job of greasing the bucketlines on the big gold boats, or from other futile experiences of trying to make a living mining gold that, at $20 or $35, always seemed undervalued. Miners knew gold not as a novelty, but as a fairly common medium; all of them had spent gold coins and some had even traded dust for their bacon and beans. To all these miners gold mining simply provided a way—often a difficult way—to make a living, or to earn some dearly needed supplementary income. They were not seeking a part in a romanticized slice of history, and certainly not looking for a pleasant way to occupy their leisure time.

But by the 1960s an entire younger generation had developed a far different perception of gold and gold mining. The post-war bust in gold mining had decimated the ranks of active miners in Colorado, leaving few with firsthand experience to explain to newcomers exactly what the profession entailed. In their place came endless motion pictures and television dramas depicting an exciting roman-ticized and sanitized version of gold mining. Instead of the shovel and sluice as the long hard means to washing out a living, Hollywood depicted the gold pan and revolver as the route to a quick fortune.

The image of the metal itself had also changed. The new genera-tion knew gold only as manufactured jewelry; they had not spent or traded gold coins, dust or nuggets, and had seen lode-gold specimens only in museum cabinets. While past generations perceived gold merely as another mineral commodity that might be profitable to mine, they saw it as the stuff of dreams—the ultimate symbol of wealth and adventure.

The post-war industrial boom also made the 1950s a decade of unprecedented economic prosperity. Steady, high-paying, five-day-per-week jobs gave Americans more leisure time than ever before and a record amount of disposable income with which to enjoy it. Simultaneously, greatly improved highways and reliable, inexpensive automobiles created a boom in western tourism. A few hours of easy driving gave tourists access to many of Colorado's remote mountain gold districts that previously were accessible only over "a hundred miles of bad road."

Sophisticated gold prospecting and small-scale gold-mining equipment also appeared in the 1950s. Most innovative was the portable metal detector, which generated considerable public interest in treasure and relic hunting, fields conceptually related to gold prospecting. Detectors originated with the mine-detecting instruments of World War II, which operated on the principle of electromagnetic induction. A primary coil-type antenna generated an electromagnetic field capable of inducing a secondary field around any conductive (metal) object within a short range. The detector's secondary, or receiving, antenna measured the strength of that secondary field, indicating its presence with a moving needle, blinking light or audio signal. Decreased size, weight and power consumption, together with improved sensitivity and range, eventually sparked consumers' interest in the instruments. By the 1960s advanced instruments were capable of detecting gold nuggets only half the size of a penny. By that time, the search for coins, relics and nuggets had brought many treasure hunters to Colorado's old gold mining districts.

The 1960s also saw portable lightweight suction dredges become available. Miners had used suction dredges to a limited extent on Colorado's placer streams since 1927, but most had been commercial-sized units with big diesel engines bolted onto six- and eight-inch industrial pumps, all floating on rafts of 55-gallon drums. But the new lightweight units used lawnmower-type gasoline engines to power one- or two-inch pumps to spew underwater gravels onto light, efficient, aluminum sluices only three feet long. For a few hundred dollars and a gallon of gasoline, anyone could dredge up mid-channel gravels that the old-timers could only reach by diverting the entire stream.

The term "recreational gold mining" was first used in the 1960s and referred only to placer mining. Lode prospecting requires at least a basic knowledge of geology, the expense of continuous assays and, for anything beyond scratching the surface of outcrops, costly core drilling or actual hardrock mining. But a recreational placer miner doesn't need the skills of a geologist or an engineer, nor the willingness to risk substantial capital. Washing gold from placer gravels requires only limited instruction, simple tools, common sense and the willingness to perform some moderate physical work—precisely the reasons it appealed to the '59ers.

Recreational gold mining had one final attraction for many Americans who were committed to their secure, but structured and predictable eight-to-five jobs. The reward for recreational gold mining went beyond the pre-taxed paycheck reward more conventional jobs offered, giving what that piece of paper ultimately represented—gold itself. Furthermore, you never knew in advance exactly how much of a reward you would receive. You faced the chance of receiving no reward at all, but also that real, yet admittedly slim, chance of striking it rich—to hit an overlooked glory hole or a pay streak loaded with dust that could pay off the car or put an addition on the house. And it was fun to dream of walking into a bank and watching the expression on the manager's face as you dropped a leather poke full of gold dust on his desk.

Initially, the general public considered recreational gold miners pleasantly eccentric, and believed Colorado's streams had little gold left. But with the image, the technology, and still undiscovered gold all in place, recreational gold mining needed only a dramatic revaluation of gold to capture the public's interest—exactly what happened in the 1970s.

Among the firsthand witnesses to the rise of recreational gold mining in Colorado was Gary Christopher. A Kansas native, Christopher studied geology at Western State College in Gunnison in the late 1950s. While other students were hitting the library, Christopher was usually in Washington Gulch, not far from Crested Butte, where placer miners worked the gravels for gold with backhoes and washing plants. At the expense of graduating with his class, he spent most of his time researching placer mining history and methods, claim-staking procedures, and the Bureau of Land Management's system of mineral-claim record keeping.

Gary Christopher eventually earned a degree, but disliked working as a company geologist. In 1976 he and his wife, Barbara, went into business for themselves, opening a metal detector shop in Englewood, just south of Denver. Soon, their shop carried fewer metal detectors and more gold-prospecting and mining equipment that better reflected Christopher's interests. The shop did a break-even business until 1979, when the price of free-market gold rocketed upward. Book sales indicated the coming boom in recreational gold mining. Almost any book with the word *gold* in the title sold out as soon as it appeared on the shelves.

The recreational gold-mining boom started in summer 1979. Christopher recalls:

> Once gold hit six hundred dollars we couldn't keep pans in stock or make dredges fast enough. During lunch hour we'd have twenty or thirty people in the shop at once. Cowboys, house-wives, truck drivers, insurance salesmen—everybody. We had guys who you knew couldn't rub two nickels together, and we had executives in patent leather shoes and four-hundred-dollar suits who couldn't tell a pick from a shovel.
>
> They bought everything that had anything to do with gold— pans, shovels, sluices, tweezers, rock picks and enough vials to hold a ton of the stuff. Manufacturers were backlogged twenty-six weeks on orders for suction dredges. When I learned I could get immediate delivery of the components, Barbara and I would work nights assembling dredges and we'd never catch up. There were probably one hundred and fifty dredges sold in Colorado in 1980, and we sold half of them. I'd guess that three-quarters of a million dollars worth of gold prospecting and amateur mining equipment was sold in Colorado that year alone. Gold hit eight hundred dollars then, and the business we did in 1980 made this shop.

*Barbara and Gary Christopher at The Prospector's Cache in Englewood. The Prospector's Cache is the largest small scale and recreational gold mining shop in the Rockies.*

Today, The Prospector's Cache is the largest retail treasure hunting and recreational gold mining shop in the entire Rocky Mountain region. The shop is located on South Broadway, only about two hundred yards from the spot where William Green Russell struck gold on Dry Creek in June 1858, then gave that sack of gravel to John Cantrell to carry east to Kansas City. Dry Creek has been bridged and rechanneled in concrete so many times that Russell and his Georgian and Cherokee miners would never recognize it. Nor would they recognize much of the stock in The Prospector's Cache, which reflects the surprising size, diversity and technological level of the recreational gold-mining industry.

At the door, visitors find a half-dozen assembled suction dredge units, complete with engines, pumps, hoses, foot valves, sluices and flotation gear; alongside lie rows of gleaming, new, lightweight aluminum sluice boxes, each with removable metal riffles and bottom matting to trap even the finest particles of gold. A long overhead rack holds two dozen metal detectors from seven different manufacturers, incorporating every conceivable discrimination, ground-cancelling and other state-of-the-art electronic adjustment feature available. With them are specialized electronic gold-seeking instruments— "nugget shooters" and resistivity meters with probes to detect deeper concentrations of conductive black sands that may contain placer gold. Of the 500 gold pans in stock, the only type a '59er would recognize are the traditional, cold-rolled steel models that range in diameter from nine to sixteen inches. The new, popular plastic pans come in green and blue colors that provide better color contrast with specks of gold and offer rims, ridges and other "gold trapping" features. The Prospector's Cache offers brass and copper pans suitable for amalgamation, and, if the customer desires something other than the traditional flat-bottomed style, the shop makes available conical steel gold pans similar to the old Spanish *batea*. For classifying gravels by every possible size, they have an extensive selection of plastic and metal sieves and screens; for "working down" sluice box concentrates, customers can choose from a variety of power, automatic, concentric wheel-type and hydraulic hydrofuge-type concentrators. Basic equipment includes miners' boots and electric cap lamps, hard hats, buckets, picks, shovels, rock picks and pry bars; more serious miners can choose from a variety of amalgamation retorts, electric ovens capable of melting gold for pouring and gold assaying, solvents and precipitating reagents. A limited selection of scuba gear is available for those wanting to take the foot valve of their suction dredge right down to the deep underwater gravels.

Hundreds of maps of every scale, compiled by the U.S. Geological Survey, U. S. Forest Service and Bureau of Land Management, as well as state agencies and commercial cartographers, detail the topography, geology and ownership status of virtually all of the mineralized areas of Colorado. The shop stocks forms and instructions for staking, recording and posting mineral claims. Five large display counters are crowded with books—pamphlets to 400-page technical tomes—at least one hundred of which have the words "gold" or "placer" in their titles. They include everything from reprints of 100-year-old classic treatments of placer mining and prospecting to original first-edition collectibles and dozens of "how-to" and "where-to" manuals. Videotapes accompanying the books cover virtually every aspect of gold and gold mining, along with related historical and environmental topics.

And, of course, the shop displays an almost cult-like array of paraphernalia to handle and study the gold once it's been found: tweezers and eye droppers to pick it up; magnets to remove magnetic black sands from the concentrates; geologist's loupes, ranging in power from 7X to 20X; pocket microscopes; pocket scales and balances; brass weights in the troy and pennyweight scales; and, finally, those sturdy, little glass vials in capacities from one-half-ounce to six ounces. The store even sells bumper stickers, including, COLORADO HAS A HEART OF GOLD AND I DIG IT.

Gary Christopher is often asked how much gold recreational gold miners actually recover. "I couldn't even guess," he admits. "Some don't find a thing. But others come back and show me what they found, or at least part of it. Then there are those who come back with a deadpan expression, say they haven't found anything, or maybe only a bit of color, yet spend a bundle on carefully selected, specialized mining equipment. The bottom line is that we're still in business, and so are other shops like us, so somebody is certainly finding some gold."

In Colorado those wanting to find placer gold can go about it in two ways: They can look for it on their own in the many miles of gold-bearing creeks and gulches, or, as some 30,000 people do each year, simply pull off the highway into one of Colorado's many well-publicized and increasingly popular fee panning areas. As many as fifty campgrounds and tourist sites offer diluted versions of the gold-panning experience. The site owners haul in gold-bearing (or salted) gravels and the guests pan at tubs and troughs. Guests pay by the pan and, at least, learn proper panning techniques while finding a bit of color.

About a half dozen of these fee panning areas offer a richer experience. Located in the historic creeks and gulches of the well-known gold districts like Central City, Black Hawk, Idaho Springs and Telluride, these sites are marked by rough-looking, hand-painted signs: GOLD PANNING—PAN YOUR OWN—GUARANTEED RESULTS—KEEP ALL YOU FIND.

One of the most popular and successful fee panning areas is Digger's Old-Timer, on Colorado Route 119 a few miles south of Black Hawk. Established in 1961, Digger's Old-Timer has been owned and operated since 1979 by Digger and Diana Cummings. Name notwithstanding, Digger Cummings was not born into gold mining, but became interested in the metal as NASA engineer with the Apollo lunar landing program, which used a considerable amount of gold in many aerospace and electronics applications. Cummings recalls:

*Each summer, recreational gold panners rework the same gravels that the '59ers washed. These panners are working at The Old-Timer, a fee panning area on the North Fork of Clear Creek near Black Hawk.*

I was really fascinated by the metal. I started doing a little panning up in the hills. When I realized how much gold was left in the creeks, I got a small sluice and went at it a little more seriously. I just stored the concentrates in jars in the garage for a couple of years. One day somebody reminded me that gold was up to three hundred dollars an ounce, and maybe I ought to find out just how much I had. When I did, I was really surprised, and became more interested in gold mining than ever. Diana and I had a chance to pick up the Old Timer and we've been showing folks how to pan gold every summer since.

Digger's Old-Timer is located in some of Colorado's most historically significant dirt, right in the channel of the North Fork of Clear Creek and just downstream from Gregory Gulch. Part of the old Hamilton claim group, the site was crossed by Colorado's first toll road and later by the narrow gauge railroad that wound up the canyon to Black Hawk and Central City. Although the miners have worked the property many times, they have left plenty of gold in the gravels. Because of its proximity to the upstream lode of origin, the site has some of Colorado's coarsest placer gold.

The Old-Timer's gravels are natural, dug right out of the alluvial banks and neither salted nor preconcentrated. Five dollars buys one hour of panning time, along with the instruction necessary to do it right. "There's color in every pan, sometimes a lot more," Cummings says. "The best one of our customers ever did was a nugget just under one troy ounce. The woman who found it let out a yell they could hear in Central City."

Digger's Old-Timer hosts about 5,000 visitors each season, from early May until late September. Over the years visitors have come from all fifty states and nearly that many foreign countries. Return customers now make up sixty percent of each season's business. Cummings says:

Gold panning gets in your blood real quick. A lot of folks are sort of skeptical at first. But when they realize that there really is gold in that dirt, and that they can wash it out as well as the next person, some just don't want to stop. I think everybody is more or less fascinated with gold, but what the gold represents is important, too. Gold panning at a place like ours is not just seeing a historical site, it's actually participating in some of that history. And the gold they find is probably the ultimate Colorado souvenir. When they bring that little vial of gold home, they're proud of it. It's not just something they bought, it's Colorado gold that they washed out themselves. Once you find that first bit of gold, it's always hard to stop because you want to know what'll be in the next pan.

145

Digger and Diana Cummings have taught gold panning to about 20,000 people, including race driver Richard Petty and his pit crew, Dr. Joyce Brothers and her family, NASA astronauts, members of the Denver Broncos and Nuggets professional sports teams, and to Britain's Princess Anne and her entourage. The Colorado Tourism Board has taped activities at the site as have dozens of television crews from all over the United States, and even from Japan and Germany. Some of Cumming's most memorable guests were blind. "That was a special tour," he explains. "We had extra instructors to work with them one-on-one. They got as much out of it was anyone else. They could feel the lighter gravels washing away, and they could feel the weight of the black sands that were left. And when they worked those down, they could press their fingers against the bits of gold. They understood exactly what was happening, because they could sense it all through their fingers. They were fascinated, you could see that in their faces."

A smaller number of far more serious recreational gold miners choose to search for gold on their own. Experienced prospectors give this advice for finding placer gold: Instead of prospecting creeks randomly, go where others have already found it. In Colorado, that encompasses a large area. Since 1858 Colorado has produced at least two million troy ounces of raw placer gold worth about $45 million, and perhaps considerably more. Colorado ranks seventh in production among the West's placer regions, far behind California's top-ranked Sierra Nevada gold belt, where placer output has topped 60 million ounces. Nevertheless, Colorado presents many opportunities for the serious recreational prospector and placer miner. Thirty-six of Colorado's sixty-three counties are officially credited with placer gold production. Some counties, including Huerfano, Garfield, Pitkin, Delta and Dolores, have only a token cumulative production of several hundred ounces. Others—Summit, Lake, Park and Clear Creek—together account for 90 percent of Colorado's total placer-gold production.

Colorado has well over one thousand miles of gold-bearing gulches, creeks, rivers and dry channels that have been subject to some type of placer mining. They range from big rivers like the Arkansas, South Platte, Blue and San Miguel to intermittent creeks only a mile or two long and wide enough to jump over. Prospectors and others have debated for decades how much gold remains in the placer gravels. They agree, however, that none have been "mined out"—that all of the original gold concentrations have never been completely exhausted. Mining has always been a complex balance of dollar value per cubic yard—which is dependent upon the price of gold—and the efficiency and cost of the recovery method. As an example, before the Fairplay Dredge shut down after the 1951 season, it was recovering 13,000 ounces of gold per year, and would have continued to do so for at least five more years had it not fallen victim to the fixed price of $35 gold.

As the old-timers say, plenty of gold waits to be mined. Dr. Ben H. Parker, Jr., in *"Gold Placers of Colorado"*, published in the *Colorado School of Mines Quarterly* in 1974, estimated that the value of contained gold in accessible deposits of "apparently workable gravels" might well amount to more than half the value of Colorado's entire placer production prior to 1957. Dr. Edgar B. Heylmun, a consulting geologist who has written extensively about the West's placer deposits for the *California Mining Journal* and other publications, states that "placer gold can be found in almost any creek or gulch which drains the Colorado Mineral Belt, and small high-grade placer deposits can still be found, even in districts which have been intensely prospected in the past." Veteran Leadville placer miner Fred Garner believes "there is probably as much gold still in the placers as has ever been taken out."

While few question that a great deal of gold remains in Colorado's placers, many are increasingly concerned about the legality of recreational gold mining. The "free land" status that the '59ers enjoyed no longer exists. Because of the General Mining Law of 1872, virtually all of Colorado's mined placer deposits are under claim or in private ownership. Nevertheless, some gold-bearing creeks are still open to claiming under the Mining Law. Some older claims, because of their claimants' failure to perform or record the required annual assessment work, have lapsed back to federal control; other claims could be contested on the same grounds. Although most U.S. Forest Service and Bureau of Land Management land remains open to mineral prospecting, claiming and recreational gold mining, these agencies have withdrawn significant areas from such use.

Many larger rivers are open to recreational mining, just as they are open to fishing, rafting and kayaking. While simple panning rarely presents a problem, the state may require permits for dredging or sluicing or may restrict these activities due to potential silt pollution during fish spawning season. Placer ground along smaller creeks, whether posted or not, is usually under claim or privately owned. The responsibility for determining land ownership status rests upon the recreational gold miner—who should never assume that other miners at work means a creek is "open."

Among the few important Colorado placer properties open to recreational gold mining are Cache Creek Park and nearby placers on the Arkansas River and Lake Creek, near the Lake-Chaffee county line and the old gold camp of Granite. Cache Creek Park has produced at least 75,000 ounces of gold and remains an active mining district, with Colorado Mined Land Reclamation permits in effect and diversion ditches built well over a century ago supplying water. Twin Lakes Associates, Inc. owns the six-square-mile property and has proposed developing the Quail Mountain Project, a downhill skiing and all-season outdoor-recreation complex. The placers remain under direct supervision of Dennis O'Neill, Twin Lakes Associates president, who has involved himself with placer mining since 1951. During the 1970s O'Neill kept the property open to a small but growing number of recreational gold miners. But by 1980 recreational gold mining had become so popular that O'Neill faced a choice: institute a few controls or close the property. O'Neill says:

> Many of Colorado's placer properties are closed to prospecting, panning, dredging and even trespassing, and any landowner will tell you why. It's because of land abuse—tree cutting, littering, hauling off gold-bearing gravels by the truckload, vandalizing old cabins and flumes, and polluting streams with commercial-size dredges.
>
> Another problem is the landowner's liability. There are some physical risks inherent to gold mining—even recreational mining. Spring runoff can make even small creeks dangerous, and early hydraulicking has created a lot of steep, unstable cliffs. Landowners can't assume liability for accidents. And if the courts ever impose that liability, believe me, there won't be a single, privately owned placer property left open to recreational gold miners in this state.

Believing recreational gold mining to be a form of outdoor recreation similar to river rafting and skiing, O'Neill decided to keep the Cache Creek Park property open. He did, however, limit the size of suction dredges to two inches, and required that miners check in first and pay a nominal fee of one dollar per day for panning and a few dollars more for sluicing or dredging. O'Neill explains:

> The fee is more of a contribution that helps us grade the roads and clean up after a season. We also know how many people are out there mining, and it gives us the chance to emphasize that they're on someone else's land and responsible for their own personal welfare.
>
> We offer recreational miners an alternative to the fee panning sites. There's a lot of land here and they're entirely on their own. There's no one looking over their shoulders. That brings back the element of prospecting, of actually choosing the dirt you want to work, and I think that's important.

About two hundred recreational gold miners come to Cache Creek Park during the April-to-October mining season, including many regulars from both Colorado and other states. O'Neill admits:

> There's only one reason they come back. That's because they find gold. But I honestly have no idea how much. If a miner finds a good pocket, he's not going tell anyone about it. Some miners show me what they've found, and it ranges from a little color to several ounces. Like anything else, the gold goes to the people who know what they're doing. I heard stories from several sources about a two and half-ounce nugget that was found along Cache Creek in 'eighty-nine. I never did see it, but I don't doubt it, either. There's a lot of gold left in those placers. If I could find the time, I'd like to look for some of it myself.

*He may never find the gold ahead . . . but what the hell . . . the search is the thing.*

—Perry Eberhart, *Treasure Tales of the Rockies*

# 9

# THE LEGENDS AND THE LOST

From wherever gold has been found come tales of gold that has been lost, and of more gold awaiting discovery. Colorado has been a fertile bed for the growth of such golden legends, for it has all the necessary elements: a huge production of gold; dark caves and forgotten mines; lofty, rugged mountains and deep, mysterious canyons; and an historically vague beginning that is itself partly based on legend. The first documented visits of the early Spanish and French adventurers were almost certainly preceded by others whose names and deeds are lost to history. Before William Green Russell made that first documented discovery of gold in 1858, other explorers had many times reported finding the metal in Colorado. We will never know how many tales are true and how much gold was found. Some reports appear to be outright fabrications. Others seem to hold various degrees of exaggeration and embellishment, for gold, perhaps more than any other material on earth, tends to expand in the retelling: colors become grains, grains become nuggets, small nuggets become big nuggets, and gold worth hundreds of dollars grows into gold worth thousands of dollars. Nevertheless, considering the richness of those shallow, bonanza placers and outcrops of visible gold that awaited the '59ers, we have to wonder how the Indians, and Spanish, the French and the American mountain men could have missed them. Indeed, when prospectors surged through the shining mountains in 1859 and 1860, they found evidence—diggings, prospect holes and even small mines—that others had sought gold there before them.

In 1961 Perry Eberhart, a *Denver Post* reporter and weekend guide at the Colorado Historical Museum in Denver, assembled a collection of 126 tales of lost treasure in Colorado. *Treasure Tales of the Rockies* enjoyed great popularity and is still available in Colorado bookstores. Eberhart made no pretense that all the tales were true. Instead, he presented them for what they were—a collection of legends, some partially substantiated, others so vague they are interesting only as folk tales. The tales range from prehistoric to twentieth century, and purport the value of the lost treasures to be from a few dollars to millions of dollars. Virtually all of Eberhart's tales share a prominent commonality: the lost treasures are usually gold.

One of Colorado's most enduring tales of lost gold is that of La Caverna del Oro—the Cave of Gold. La Caverna del Oro, also known as Spanish Cave, is one of the Marble Caves, a group of natural limestone caverns located at the 11,500-foot-level of 13,262-foot high Marble Mountain, on the eastern side of the Sangre de Cristo (Blood of Christ) Range. Although Marble Mountain has never been a mining district, small prospects of copper and uranium have been found. The discovery of gold in the 1890s caused a minor rush to Crestone, only six miles to the west across the crest of the range.

Legends of lost gold in the Sangre de Cristos originated with the early Spanish, who probably first reached Colorado by following the Rio Grande valley north from their New Mexican settlements. Legend tells us that the first Spanish visitor may have been a mysterious Father de la Cruz, who split from the Coronado expedition in 1541, eventually finding gold in the Sangre de Cristos. Tales from the New Mexican settlements since that time, often mention "rich gold mines to the north."

La Caverna del Oro apparently came to the attention of English-speaking immigrants in 1869, when Captain Elisha P. Horn, an early settler of the nearby Wet Mountain Valley, found a Maltese cross painted on a rock high on the side of Marble Mountain. The faded, obviously old cross marked the entrance to a natural cave, several hundreds of yards below which Horn found the stuff of which legends are made—human remains and rusted armor, apparently of Spanish origin.

J. H. Yeoman made the next visit of note in 1879, reporting his observations in the *Denver Republican* on February 20, 1880:

> . . . at the foot of the mountain, which is penetrated by caves, is a ancient fort, the entrance of which seems to guard the

*The Maltese cross that appeared on a rock near an entrance to La Caverna del Oro. In this photograph, taken in the 1960s, vandals had destroyed a portion of the cross.*

*The entrance to La Caverna del Oro is located at an elevation of 11,500 feet on Marble Mountain. The Maltese cross can be seen just below the center of the photograph.*

153

entrance of the cave. The walls of the fort are made of rocks and timbers and must have been built many years ago.

In 1920 two U.S. Forest Service Rangers, Paul Gilbert and Arthur Carhart, investigated La Caverna del Oro and interviewed Apollina Apodaca, a 102-year-old woman who claimed direct descent from the early Spanish explorers and settlers of the San Luis Valley. Apodaca stated that when she was a child (about 1830), the Spanish had already mined gold from La Caverna del Oro, which was then called *La Mina de los Tres Pasos*, or the Three Steps Mine. An internal shaft descended one hundred feet, from which point the Spanish miners tunneled back into the mountain. Even deeper was a set of heavy timber doors concealing the vein source of the gold. Apodaca recalled tales of enslaved Indian miners revolting, forcing the Spanish into the lower caves. But after several days, the trapped Spanish made their way underground to the upper entrance. Using the advantage of surprise and higher ground, they finally emerged to kill the Indians.

The rangers later explored the caves, finding a rusted shovel, lengths of rotted hemp rope, and a deep internal shaft which blocked further passage. Their discoveries attracted the interest of *Denver Post* publisher Frederick Bonfils, one of Colorado's most respected citizens, who mounted his own expedition. On August 11, 1929, *The Denver Post* printed this intriguing account:

> . . . The main cave is on the side of a deep, steep gully, which is filled with an immense snowpack until about the first of August. The snow, many feet deep, completely covers the cave mouth; it was only in the last few days that one could reach the hole.
>
> The opening is a jagged affair about five feet high and two feet wide. It would scarcely be noticed if one had not been instructed to search for the cross painted in dull red on the rocks near the right of the opening. This emblem, about two feet square, has the perfect form of a German "iron cross."
>
> No person living in the region today knows who painted that cross upon the mountainside. It is very old. It was old when the first white settler saw it more than sixty years ago.
>
> . . . the tunnel suddenly opened into a quite spacious chamber. The floor dropped away in a sheer precipice and was covered with ice a foot thick at the brink.
>
> Wedged between the stone walls at the brink of this drop was an ancient log, to which was fastened an iron-chain ladder that disappeared down the shaft. The log was badly rotted, and the chain too rusted to bear a person's weight. We could not hazard

a guess as to how long this former means of descent had hung there.

At a depth of fifty feet, we came to a shelf—more properly a twist in the shaft. Here a very narrow opening had to be passed, and we had no more rope on which to proceed. Shining our torches down this hole, we could only see the illimitable blackness. . . .

La Caverna del Oro was back in the headlines again a few years later, this time due to an expedition led by Pete Moser, an experienced Colorado gold prospector. This description of Moser's remarkable discovery appeared in the *Rocky Mountain News* on September 4, 1932:

### SKELETON FOUND CHAINED BY NECK
### IN COLORADO MYSTERY CAVE

. . . on the end of a rope [Peter Moser] was lowered away into the forbidding and unknown depths beneath him. Foot after foot he scraped along the rock side of the cave. It seemed the bottom would never be reached. Finally he touched ground. His companions had laid out 250 feet of rope. . . . With a lighter rope they lowered a lantern.

Forty feet downward they saw the bottom, and in the light of the lantern could clearly make out a skeleton.

With a metal strap encircling the neck, the pile of bones reclined against the rocky walls, as if the person who died there had been chained in a sitting position and left to starve.

. . . On the second level they found evidence of crude timbering and at the top of the second shaft was an old tree trunk fitted together until it formed a crude windlass. Evidence enough to indicate that out of these black depths slaves had hoisted riches for the Spaniards . . .

That report attracted the attention of some of Colorado's most experienced spelunkers, along with Dr. LeRoy Hafen, curator of the Colorado Historical Society archives and museum. But by the time their quickly mounted expedition reached the site only weeks later someone had apparently detonated several dynamite charges in a futile effort to seal the cave. Hafen's group was unable to find the skeleton Pete Moser had reported, but they did discover a crude, hand-forged hammer, which Dr. Hafen declared to be of seventeenth century origin.

If the credibility of the legend had not yet been established by these discoveries and reports, La Caverna del Oro received what every legend needs—a feature article in *The New York Times*, which ran on October 2, 1932:

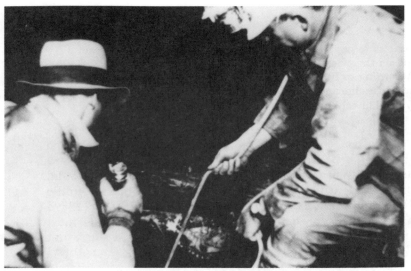

*Treasure hunters and underground explorers searching La Caverna del Oro in one of the well publicized expeditions of the early 1930s.*

OLD GOLD MINE FOUND IN SOUTHERN COLORADO

EXPLORING PARTY BELIEVES IT IS OF INDIAN
ORIGIN AND KNOWN TO EARLY SPANIARDS.

DENVER, Sept. 29.—The discovery of a skeleton chained to a rock at a deep level in the Sangre de Cristo Mountains in southern Colorado had prompted an exploration of this territory which, according to legends of the Southwest Indians, was once worked for gold deposits by Spanish explorers. Pete Moser, a Denver prospector, discovered the skeleton after a Maltese cross painted on a ledge had indicated that other prospectors had been there.

The exploring party, consisting of Dr. LeRoy Hafen, Historical Society, Carl Blaurock and Orville Hough, Colorado Mountain Club Members, has made a preliminary survey. They found an ancient windlass which probably was used by the Spaniards or other early workers of the mine. At the level 110 feet below the point where the windlass was found, there was a large room with several tunnels leading in as many different directions. A hand forged hammer of ancient manufacture was found in the room.

It is believed this is the mine from which the Spaniards obtained their gold. According to stories of the Pecos Indians, a Spanish priest, Father La Cruz, decoyed Indians to the place and then forced them to work the mine until he had enough gold to weigh down three mules. The Indians were slain and the priest left with his gold. He was never seen again, but in 1853

156

several nuggets were found not far from the mine, where it was supposed the priest had been slain.

According to Indian legend, the cave was known before the Spaniards came and from it the Indians obtained the gold which they used lavishly for ceremonial vessels. . . .

A small rush of hardy, determined treasure hunters followed, the welfare of whom concerned both the Colorado Mountain Club and the Custer County Sheriff. Although no one reported any important new discoveries, the explorations continued for decades. Explorers found bone fragments, identified as being from deer, elk and buffalo, in the cave in 1959, and found several new entrances a year later. Lloyd Paris, in *Caves of Colorado*, calls La Caverna del Oro the most dangerous cave on Marble Mountain; other experts call it "the worst cave in Colorado," because of the vertical drops, low temperatures, high humidity, and, should an accident occur, its inaccessibility and remoteness. Spelunkers face a real possibility of becoming lost; mapped sections include 3,500 feet of twisting passages with a vertical drop of over 700 feet, and many yet unmapped passages exist. La Caverna del Oro is a cave best left to the more experienced, but explorers will doubtlessly continue their search, finding new passages, and perhaps someday the beam of a spelunker's light will fall upon heavy timbers of an ancient door.

Only ten miles south of La Caverna del Oro lies another of Colorado's topographical features suited for legends of lost gold—the Great Sand Dunes. The wind-deposited sand dunes cover seventy

*Medano Creek flows by the edge of Colorado's Great Sand Dunes. The area is rich in gold-related legend and was the site of a brief, ill-fated gold rush in the early 1930s.*

square miles at the eastern edge of the San Luis Valley at the base of the Sangre de Cristo Range. As high as 700 feet and almost devoid of vegetation, the great dunes shift with the wind, actually moving as far as 400 feet per year. The legends of lost gold in the dunes seem to have developed about the same time as the legend of La Caverna del Oro. A later story reports gold in decaying sacks being found in 1853 at San Luis Lake, a large, salty depression just east of the dunes, a tale that seems related to the mysterious Father de la Cruz. Stories of early prospectors support the tales of gold at both La Caverna del Oro and the Great Sand Dunes, for ancient diggings were found in the mountain canyons just east of the dunes.

The early settlers of the San Luis Valley pursued farming, not mining. The farmers explored the barren dunes, sometimes finding relics, remains of wagons, and even human and horse bones, all of which the shifting sands covered and uncovered. At the northeast edge of the dunes, they found an eerie dead forest of ponderosa pines that had fallen victim to the relentless advance of the dunes.

Many legends evolved about the Great Sand Dunes. Some were humorous, telling of horses that grew webbed feet to survive in their sandy environment. Some were ominous, including stories about entire towns disappearing beneath the shifting sands. And still others told of gold, most often a "Spanish ox cart" laden with gold bars that the Spanish had hauled down from mines high in the Sangre de Cristos, only to have it swallowed by the marching dunes. From time to time, the winds uncovered the ox cart with its burden of gold, usually at last light—only to cover it again beneath the sands by dawn.

The legends were given a ring of truth when prospectors found natural gold in dune sand in the late 1920s. One of the mineral constituents of the sand is magnetite, the common magnetic oxide of iron—familiar to placer miners as one of the black sands in pan and sluice concentrates. Wind movement of the sand concentrated the magnetite in long dark streaks beneath the crests of the lee side of the dunes. In 1928 assays of the magnetite streaks revealed the presence of extremely fine particles of flour gold. Although the gold was present only in trace amounts, the news hit the papers as a big "strike," with this description of the "gold-bearing sands" appearing in the *Pueblo Chieftain:* "The sand, which has a large mineral content, is of a clear gray color, has been tested and found to have in it gold running $3 to the ton."

A horde of prospectors arrived to hammer down their claim stakes—most of which the sand soon buried—while promoters calculated the extent of the new bonanza. Multiplying the best assay report grades by wild estimates of the volume of sand present, they concluded, and newspapers reported, that nearly 300 million ounces of gold worth $5.9 billion was waiting to be washed out of the Great Sand Dunes. And the dunes were advertised as a miner's dream—an enormous deposit that required no digging through deep barren overburden, no drilling and blasting, and no hauling and crushing. Some miners set up sluices in the bed of Medano Creek, only to find them high and dry in the morning, after Medano, a classic example of a disappearing river, changed course or dried up overnight. The most ambitious effort to mine the dunes came in 1932, when the Volcanic Mining Company built a small mill with amalgamation tables capable of recovering the extremely fine particles of gold. But the Volcanic Mining Company and all the other efforts failed, because the wild promotion was based only on invalid sampling of the assay material. When cooler heads finally prevailed, the gold content of the dunes was shown to be only slightly higher than normal geochemical background levels.

Meanwhile, San Luis Valley residents, concerned that a gold rush would jeopardize the beauty and tourism potential of the dunes, petitioned the Department of the Interior for help. Late in 1932 President Herbert Hoover proclaimed the dunes a National Monument. Although the designation prohibited all further prospecting and mining, the legends of gold survived. As late as the 1960s, after winter storms had resculpted the great dunes, the shifting sands uncovered, then covered again, what several individuals described as an ancient ox cart.

Early visits of the French to aptly named Treasure Mountain, south of Wolf Creek Pass and near the headwaters of the San Juan River in Rio Grande County, form the basis for another of Colorado's great legends of lost gold. In 1790 a well-equipped French expedition supposedly left St. Louis for the Rockies, which Spain then claimed. With 300 men and 450 horses, the venture sounds suspiciously like a French version of Coronado's epic journey of 1541-42. The story lacks documentation, but the French appeared to know exactly where they were going.

Arriving near Treasure Mountain, the French began systematically mining rich, gold-bearing vein outcrops, melting and pouring their recovered gold into bars. Because of the high elevation, they worked only during the summers, wintering near the Spanish settlements at Taos. In 1793, after disease and privation had reduced their ranks to 100, the French made preparations to leave. But Indian trouble followed and the French left their gold behind. Of the handful of Frenchmen who returned to the Mississippi, only one ever made it back to France. He prepared two maps of the mining site from memory, depositing one with the government, and retaining the other for his family.

About 1830 a small group of Frenchmen attempted to return to the mines, then in Mexican territory. At Taos, they hired a guide, Bernando Sanchez. Apparently unable to locate the mines, they returned to Taos, reoutfitted, and set out again the following year. This time, Sanchez returned alone, claiming Indians had slaughtered the entire party. However, many Mexicans believed that the French had paid off Sanchez to keep him quiet, and that they had removed the gold from Mexican territory by another route. Others suspected him of murder.

But later reports told of Indians with French equipment and weapons, and that Sanchez himself had returned alone to search for the mines. Stories also report that about 1860, just after the Pike's Peak rush, a Frenchman appeared with an original copy of the map, but he, too, was unsuccessful in locating the mines. As late as the 1960s, prospectors and ranchers from Pagosa Springs still searched for the mines, most often near the headwaters of the San Juan River. Prospectors have ambitiously dug some shafts up to sixty feet deep. No one, however, has reported finding the old French mines.

We could easily dismiss the entire tale as being high on intrigue but woefully short on documentation except for the bonanza veins of gold discovered in 1873 at Summitville, only five miles southeast of the San Juan headwaters. Interestingly, the earliest American prospectors report older diggings, leading us to wonder if Frenchmen in the 1790s first mined the gold-bearing outcrops that eventually made Summitville famous.

Some of Colorado's tales of lost gold are more thoroughly documented, including the story of Jim Reynolds and his band of Southern sympathizers who raised havoc in the South Park goldfields in 1863-64. Jim Reynolds first rode north out of Texas in 1863, into the Civil War tensions of Colorado Territory. Reynolds and a small gang wandered about the gold camps near Fairplay, never working, yet always riding good horses and spending money freely. Not surprisingly, locals soon suspected them of a number of petty robberies in the area. But when Reynolds tried a bigger job—the gold shipment on a Fairplay-Denver stage—he was apprehended and imprisoned in Denver. Somehow, Reynolds broke out and returned to Texas.

During the winter of 1863-64 Reynolds developed a patriotic fervor. We'll never know if Reynolds was serious about capturing Colorado gold for the Confederacy, or whether he used patriotism to justify and perhaps glorify his budding career as a highwayman.

Either way, he promoted himself to the rank of "Colonel," recruited a gang of twenty members, issued an oath of allegiance to the Confederacy, and even gave himself a suitable nickname—Jim "The Bold" Reynolds.

The gang slowly worked its way back to Colorado in spring 1864, stopping first to knock off a wagon train in New Mexico. By the time the gang arrived in South Park, its numbers had dwindled to eight. Although their first jobs were small, Reynolds made his presence known by informing his victims that "One Thousand Texas Rangers" were on their way to capture Colorado gold, and to "burn Denver to the ground." Reynolds successfully raised fears of a Confederate "invasion." The *Rocky Mountain News* reported that governor John Evans was packing a gun on the Denver streets, and even Catholic priests in the San Luis Valley armed themselves. But the braggadocio proved a big mistake—Jim "The Bold" Reynolds had seriously underestimated the intensity of wartime sentiment in Colorado Territory.

On July 26, 1864 the Reynolds gang pulled the job that put them in the history books. At McLaughlin's Station, ten miles east of Fairplay, they robbed a McClellan-Spotswood stage bound for Denver. The loot included raw placer gold, three cans of amalgam, personal valuables, and a sack of U. S. mail containing some greenback currency. The robbery netted the gang perhaps $7,000. Riding well ahead of word of the robbery, Reynolds led his men east to the Kenosha House for a celebratory meal, then to the Omaha House for a good night's rest, and finally into hiding in the hills near Kenosha Pass.

Among the robbery victims was a Fairplay prostitute who had mailed $200 to her mother in Illinois. Informed of the loss, she screamed, "If the men of this town had any guts, they'd go after those bastards!" They certainly did. Three posses totalling sixty men, each armed to the teeth, set out after the "guerillas." Jack Sparks' posse from Breckenridge found them holed up in Handcart Gulch. After a confused nighttime shoot-out, the gang scattered, but Sparks found the body of Owen Singletary, Reynolds' right-hand man. Posse member Dr. George Cooper used his surgical skills to decapitate the unfortunate Singletary, preserving his head in alcohol for public display in Fairplay and Alma.

Only two members of the gang, including John Reynolds, brother of Jim "The Bold," escaped into New Mexico. The rest rode for their lives across South Park just ahead of the posses, which now numbered seventy-five men supported by supply wagons. Jim Reynolds and the few men he had left, hungry, weary from lack of sleep, and with their horses exhausted, gave up without a fight near Canon City.

The posses triumphantly hauled Reynolds and his men to Denver, where the citizens, riding a growing wave of anti-Southern sentiment, wanted blood. The *Rocky Mountain News* wanted it, too, as shown in this inflammatory article on August 20, 1864:

### GUERILLAS BROUGHT IN

Marshall Hunt & posse arrived here this morning with 9 prisoners whom they placed in irons in the Marshall's jail. This number comprises 6 horse thieves & c., captured at a point on the Arkansas River and in the South Park, as well as that inhuman fiend Reynolds, the merciless, murdering, marauder and rebel chief who led that band in the mountains, robbed McClellan's mail coach & c. A general feeling, outbursts of revenge based along upon retributive justice, has been expressed today, and still is slumbering to soon burst forth in bold volcanic flames of wrath and indignation, to this effect—that this insatiate felon, this defiant thief, assassin, highwayman and outlaw, ought to be furnished with the shortest prayer in the Litany and strung up as high as Harran, to expiate his life of atrocity and bloody crime.

Exactly what to do with the Reynolds gang was a legal question that the authorities had to answer quickly, due to growing fear of a lynch mob. They decided to consider them soldiers, turning them over, accordingly, to the Third Colorado Cavalry. The Volunteers gave the gang a quick secret trial in which they were convicted of conspiracy against the United States and sentenced to hang. Concerned that they exceeded their authority, the Volunteers immediately moved to get the prisoners out of Denver, first to "safe" custody at Fort Lyon, then out of the territory to Fort Leavenworth for execution. But the *Rocky Mountain News*, as the prisoners prepared to depart, echoed its call for swift "justice" on September 5:

Captain Cree's Company took Jim Reynolds and 4 or 5 of his guerilla partners away from the U.S. Marshall's charge on Saturday, to place them in safe custody in Fort Lyon, subject to further orders from the Commander of the Department. A good crowd convened about the jail to see the culprits start, expressing the hope that rations of ball and buckshot might be dealt out to them on general principles and before they reached their destination.

The mention of "ball and buckshot" was, unfortunately for the Reynolds gang and shamefully for Colorado Territory, a portent. Captain Cree apparently moved his charges only to the old camp of

Russellville, near the head of Cherry Creek, forty miles south of Denver. On September 9, 1864 the *Rocky Mountain News* offered this account of what followed:

### THE REYNOLDS BAND

We probably never again shall have occasion to mention the Reynolds Guerilla Band except as a thing of the past.

. . . Last Saturday morning the prisoners were placed in charge of Co. A, 3rd Cav. for removal to Fort Lyon. On the road, we learn, that they were impudent and insulting to the soldiers and abused all the Colorado Volunteers. At California Ranch they were especially abusive and insolent. Captain Cree was obliged to interfere and send his men away, after which he warned the prisoners that they must treat his soldiers with respect or he could not answer for the consequences; that they had already made them so angry he could hardly control them.

Beyond the point named a few miles, at the old Russellville townsite, the wagon containing the prisoners and its guard had fallen 50 or 60 rods behind the command, when they halted to water their horses. Whilst doing so, the prisoners made a concerted attempt to escape, when they were fired upon by the the guard and all instantly killed.

"Uncle Dick" Wootton, the famed trapper, trader, scout and Indian fighter offered a far different account of what transpired on the plains that September day in 1864. In Howard Louis Conard's *"Uncle Dick" Wootton*, the frontiersman told this story about what he saw while accompanying the family of a deceased friend from Pueblo to Denver:

The lady and children by the way, were very much shocked by a discovery which we made, as we drove along the road between where the town of Colorado Springs is now, and Denver. We noticed the ravens hovering about a spot not far from the road; in a small grove, and driving to once side, we found there the skeletons of four men, bound with ropes to as many trees. The flesh had been picked clean from the bones, but a bullet hole in each skull showed how the men had met their death. Each skeleton stood in a pair of boots, which was all that was left of them in the way of clothing, and altogether this was as ghastly a find, along a lonely road, as one could imagine. We learned afterwards that the skeletons were those of the notorious "Jim" Reynolds and three of his band of robbers, who had been captured and summarily executed only a short time ago.

No one investigated the incident, but the Reynolds story was not put to rest. In 1871 John Reynolds, Jim "The Bold's" brother, returned to Colorado. Still a highwayman at heart, and with the same

163

bad luck, John Reynolds was mortally wounded trying to steal horses. Before he died, he told his partner, Albert Brown, that the loot from the 1864 stage robbery was buried in Handcart Gulch. One of the prisoners had apparently also told that story before his execution. The gang had buried the loot, or at least most of it, a few miles above Reynolds' main camp in Handcart Gulch, near a timberline spruce marked by a knife. Jim Reynolds himself had driven a knife, crudely fashioned from a file into the tree, broken off the point, then driven the point deeper ahead of the blade. His idea, supposedly, was that if the knife were removed, the point would remain in the tree.

None of this information helped Albert Brown, for he is believed to have died a destitute drunk in Wyoming. About 1900 an elderly man named Tex Taylor arrived in South Park. He claimed to be the uncle of the gang member who had escaped the posses along with John Reynolds and he had a crude map of Handcart Gulch, showing a stone barricade guarding a steep trail, the main campsite in an aspen grove and, just beyond it, a log corral. A mile and a half above the camp was a large spruce, and under it the shallow grave of a gang member who had taken a bullet. According to the map, the gold was buried nearby.

Taylor didn't find the gold, either, but the story was back in the news in 1933 when Vernon Crow, a prospector living in Handcart Gulch, found a knife handle protruding from a long-dead timberline spruce. Working the handle, he extracted a crude dagger made from a file, with its point missing. In 1938 Crow found old stone breastworks and the decaying aspen logs of a corral above a small clearing in an aspen park. The next year he noticed a strange mark carved on an old spruce and, nearby, a rock set upright in the ground. Investigating further, Vernon Crow found a shallow grave with the remains of a man who had been buried with his boots on.

In 1949 the postmistress of nearby Grant, a one-time stage station on the Denver-Fairplay trail, commented on the number of treasure hunters who had searched for the Reynolds gold. "There must be a treasure up there somewhere," she said. "All sorts of clues have been found. One old man [Crow] who lives up there has found lots of clues, but even he can't find the exact spot. Why, during the war, you'd be surprised just how many soldiers came up here on their furloughs to dig."

Today, Handcart Gulch still attracts the treasure hunters. Five miles east of Kenosha Pass, a dirt road turns off U.S. Route 285, and five miles further along the North Fork of the South Platte River is the old town site of Hall Valley. The Handcart Gulch trail, well marked by U. S. Forest Service signs, leads into the gulch itself, where you can still find the stone breastworks, the clearing in the

164

aspen grove and the remains of Vernon Crow's cabin. Still further, the gulch broadens into a timberline basin, from which the trail crosses the Continental Divide at Webster Pass. Near timberline are many old, shallow potholes, testimony to those who have searched for the stolen gold of Jim "The Bold" Reynolds. The loot—the raw placer gold, the amalgam and the rest of it—could easily be worth $50,000 today. And, even if the gold isn't there, some say you'll still find your reward just by searching for it.

That idea goes back for centuries. It was advanced by the chronicler of the Coronado expedition, who wrote in 1545, "Although they found not the gold for which they sought, better still, they found a place in which to search." In *Treasure Tales of the Rockies*, Perry Eberhart said the same thing, if a bit more colloquially. "He may never find the gold ahead," Eberhart wrote of all gold seekers, "but, what the hell . . . the search is the thing."

*Certainly our Colorado gold collection is quite valuable. But that's not the point, because no one can really place a value on heritage. And our gold collection—historically, mineralogically and aesthetically—represents a big part of the heritage of Colorado.*

—Jack Murphy, Curator of Geology
Denver Museum of Natural History, March, 1991

# 10

# PRESERVING THE HERITAGE

The world's generic gold supply has swallowed virtually all of the estimated 42 million troy ounces—1,439 standard tons—of gold mined in Colorado since 1858. Only a miniscule fraction of Colorado's gold has escaped the stamp and grinding mills, the smelters, and the amalgamation, chlorination and cyanidation processes to retain its original form and identity. That natural gold amounts to only a few thousand ounces, but most is of unusual size, mineralogical form, geologic origin and beauty, and of historic significance.

Unfortunately, little of the gold mined during the Pike's Peak rush exists as specimens. Placer miners doubtlessly mined nuggets considerably larger than those known today, and took extraordinary lode specimens from the rich outcrops, only to send them to the stamp mills. The idea of preserving specimens was contrary to the spirit and goals of the gold rush participants. Most prospectors and miners knew only a hand-to-mouth existence, and gold, in whatever form or size, was merely the means to the picks, shovels, bacon and beans that would make possible the search for that bigger bonanza waiting just over the next ridge.

The first specimens of Colorado gold to be preserved were saved for promotional purposes in the late 1860s, and displayed in the East to attract development capital. Preservation of specimens for rarity and beauty was unknown in Colorado until the 1880s, when spectacular crystallized gold poured from the narrow, erratic veins of Farncomb

Hill. By the 1890s mine owners including John F. Campion were amassing personal collections of natural gold, and United States Geological Survey field investigators including Samuel F. Emmons and Frederick Leslie Ransome were describing notable specimens in reports that later became classics of field geology. Meanwhile, enormously popular regional, national and international trade expositions and World's Fairs provided a forum for competitive display of gold specimens.

Initially, appraisers assigned monetary values only minimally higher than the bullion value of the contained gold to even the most remarkable specimens of natural gold. After 1900, however, a growing number of wealthy serious collectors competed to acquire fine specimens, the availability of which decreased as mines turned to lower grade ores. Because of supply and demand, as well as an increased mineralogical and aesthetic appreciation, the "collector value" of gold specimens began increasing substantially. Almost all the finest specimens of natural Colorado gold that exist today passed first into private collections, then, fortunately, to museums across the nation.

The Natural History Museum of Los Angeles County, in Los Angeles, California, has over sixty specimens of Colorado gold from twelve counties. Among the finest are a wire gold ram's horn from the Ground Hog Mine, gold-in-quartz from Leadville's Little Jonny and Telluride's Smuggler-Union, and several pieces of crystallized gold from Farncomb Hill near Breckenridge.

The regular collection of the American Museum of Natural History in New York City contains fifty-one specimens of Colorado gold, with twenty-seven more specimens in a collection recently acquired from Columbia University. Most notable is a 14.8-troy-ounce crystallized gold sponge from Leadville's Little Jonny. Many of the pieces in the regular collection passed from John F. Campion to William Boyce Thompson, founder of the Newmont Mining Corporation, currently the nation's largest gold producer. Thompson's private collection, assembled in the early 1900s, included over two hundred troy ounces of crystallized gold, most from the Little Jonny. Upon his death in 1927, Thompson bequeathed his entire collection to the American Museum of Natural History.

The Smithsonian Institution's National Museum of Natural History in Washington, D. C., has eighty specimens of Colorado gold, including a two- by three-inch plate of galena cubes encrusted with small gold crystals from Central City; a 26.43-troy-ounce mass of gold crystals from Leadville; and a six-by-three-inch group of flat gold crystals from Farncomb Hill weighing 20.25 troy ounces.

The Harvard Mineralogical Museum at Harvard University in Cambridge, Massachusetts, also has an extensive collection of Colorado gold, including one specimen of extraordinary significance—the eight-troy ounce ram's horn found in 1887 at the Ground Hog Mine, near Red Cliff in Eagle County. This specimen was owned first by one of the mine owners, then by a Denver collector, and finally by Professor W. P. Blake, a nationally prominent collector. When Blake died in 1912, Alfred Burrage, a Harvard alumnus and copper-mining magnate, acquired the piece, helping him to assemble one of the world's premier gold collections. When the Burrage bequeathed his collection to Harvard University in 1948, the ram's horn, then recognized as the largest known wire-gold specimen in the world, went on public display for the first time. When the price of free-market gold began soaring in the 1970s, the Harvard museum became increasingly concerned with the security of the irreplaceable piece. By 1980 they had withdrawn the ram's horn from display and locked it in a bank vault.

Much of the best Colorado gold, however, has remained right at home. The Colorado School of Mines, in Golden, has 120 specimens of Colorado gold, including the eighty pieces of the Frank C. Allison collection, permanently displayed in a vault in the lobby of the Arthur Lakes Library. The Allison collection, interestingly, narrowly escaped the melting pot. Frank C. Allison operated a popular cigar store in a Denver hotel for decades, slowly acquiring a substantial private collection of natural gold from Colorado and several foreign mining districts. After the Depression, Allison fell upon hard financial times and was forced to sell the gold. He delivered it to Charles O. Porter, one of Denver's leading assayers, to be melted down. Porter, who had seen plenty of gold in his time, realized that these specimens deserved a better fate. On his own, Porter contacted the Boettchers, successful investment brokers and one of Colorado's wealthiest families, and asked them to consider purchasing gold. Charles and Claude K. Boettcher did so, then immediately donated the entire Allison collection to the Colorado School of Mines. Donating the Allison collection was one of the first philanthropic gestures leading the family to found the Boettcher Foundation.

Top specimens displayed at the Colorado School of Mines include a large intricate mass of leaf gold from the Smuggler-Union, crystallized gold-on-quartz from Leadville, wire and crystallized gold from Farncomb Hill, and high-grade calaverite from Cripple Creek's Independence Mine. Exhibits at the nearby Geology Museum include a replica of an underground mine, and a bullion balance dating from 1859 upon which some sixteen tons of Colorado gold was weighed.

The most recently assembled collection of Colorado gold may be seen in the Gold Rush Room of the National Mining Hall of Fame and Museum in Leadville. The museum displays relics, historical photographs, and both placer and lode specimens from the seventeen states that have hosted gold rushes. In 1989 the newly established museum exhibited one of Colorado's most famous gold specimens—that eight-troy ounce ram's horn that was mined in 1887 only twenty miles away at the Ground Hog Mine near Red Cliff. The Harvard Mineralogical Museum loaned the world's largest known piece of wire gold after the museum made elaborate security preparations, including installing a sophisticated electronic alarm system wired directly into the Lake County Sheriff's Office three blocks away. When discovered, newspapers noted the specimen had "an increased value due to its curious and rare formation." In 1989 the specimens' insurance coverage reflected that "increased value." While the Leadville museum displayed the ram's horn they had it insured for $750,000—about $95,000 per ounce.

In 1991 the National Mining Hall of Fame & Museum acquired the private collection of Colorado residents Dick and Mary Bowman. For many years the Bowman collection of Colorado gold was a familiar sight in a display vault in the United Bank of Denver. The most notable piece is a bright, compact, 23-troy-ounce mass of crystallized gold from Leadville's Little Jonny Mine. When mined in 1892 the beautiful mass of gold had been shoveled into an ore car and was headed for the stamp mills before it was noticed. Other top pieces include a group of unusually formed Leadville nuggets; four 1½-ounce nuggets from Fairplay; an eight-inch-long, cut-and-polished piece of rich gold-in-quartz from the Camp Bird; wire gold from Farncomb Hill; clusters of delicate leaf gold on white quartz from Idaho Springs' Dixie Mine; high-grade sylvanite from the Cresson Mine; and other Cripple Creek sylvanite specimens in both the "light roast" and "dead roast" reduction stages.

The museum also displays industrial bullion balances; small, handmade "pocket" balances used by the '59ers at Central City; an acrylic painting depicting Fred and Eileen Garner at work in one of Colorado's last "mom and pop" placer mining operations; and a detailed, technically accurate 22-scene diorama created by Hank Gentsch of Denver, showing every type of mining method and equipment ever employed at Central City.

Although little, if any, of the gold mined during the Pike's Peak rush exists in its natural form, some is displayed in fabricated form—the "Pike's Peak" gold coins minted in the early 1860s, when the government allowed private minting. The Colorado History Museum of the Historical Society of Colorado has six of the Clark, Gruber & Co. 1860-61 issues in four denominations, and three sets of dies and reproductions of the gold coins J. J. Conway & Co. minted in Summit County during the same era.

In Colorado Springs, the American Numismatic Association World Money Museum collection has replicas of the J. J. Conway & Company gold coins, and gold coins and patterns (gilded copper) of Clark, Gruber & Company. *A Guide Book of United States Coins* (1990) values the Clark, Gruber & Co. $10 Pike's Peak gold coin of 1860, containing one-half-troy-ounce of gold, as high as $16,000. The World Money Museum also displays a 10,000-troy-ounce beam balance manufactured about 1900 by the Bureau of the Mint, canvas high-grade ore sacks, assaying equipment and high-grade ore from Cripple Creek, and a number of fine gold nuggets from Alma.

The world's premier collection of Colorado gold belongs to the Denver Museum of Natural History, in Denver, Colorado. Among the gifts instrumental in founding the museum was John F. Campion's entire private collection of gold from his mines near Breckenridge. Campion also served as the first president of the museum's Board of Trustees.

The museum displays superb gold specimens representing over a century of Colorado mining in the subdued lighting of the triple-security Gold and Silver Room, the main attraction of the museum's Coors Mineral Hall. Most of the Campion collection, which contains over six hundred specimens of leaf, wire and arborescent forms of crystallized gold, are now on exhibit. The highlight of the collection is "Tom's Baby," the remarkable mass of crystallized gold mined at Farncomb Hill in 1887.

When the Denver Museum of Natural History received the Campion collection in 1900, Jefferson Hurley's *Famous Gold Nuggets of the World* listed "Tom's Baby". The museum displayed the specimen for several years; then, somehow, it disappeared, both from display as well as from the museum's inventory. Memories of "Tom's Baby" were kept alive only by a few Colorado historians, among them *Rocky Mountain News* writer Pasquale Marranzino. In a 1955 editorial, Marranzino observed, "The cloak of Colorado history, and the dim light of time, keep hiding the fact that someone kidnapped 'Tom's Baby.'"

In 1971 the Rev. Mark Fiester, a historian from the town of Frisco, took up the trail while researching *Blasted, Beloved Breckenridge*. Fiester confirmed that "Tom's Baby" was no longer on the museum's inventory, but also learned that the museum displayed only a part of the Campion collection, with the remainder long secured in a Denver bank vault. A subsequent inventory of the vault did not uncover "Tom's Baby" per se but it turned up many Campion gold specimens, including two large pieces weighing 78 and 24 troy ounces. Those pieces fit together perfectly to match the photograph of the original "Tom's Baby" in Hurley's *Famous Gold Nuggets of the World*. After further investigation, museum officials concluded that several other pieces in the Campion collection accounted for the "missing" 34 troy ounces of the original specimen.

Museum specialists had apparently broken "Tom's Baby" when they used acid to remove its oxide matrix in preparation for display. For several reasons—the physical alteration, lack of historical background and little appreciation of the specimen's significance, as well as concerns about security—the museum consigned the pieces of "Tom's Baby" to the bank vault during the 1920s, where they remained, largely forgotten, until their rediscovery in 1972. Today, "Tom's Baby," Colorado's finest specimen of lode gold, is back on display. The reassembled, 102-troy-ounce piece provides viewers with an unforgettable reminder of the days when Farncomb Hill gave up one of the world's greatest treasures in crystallized gold.

Another specimen with special significance is the seventeen-pound piece of rich gold-in-quartz mined in the 1880s from the Smuggler-Union. The original owner, coal mining magnate John A. Porter, donated the piece to the Colorado Scientific Society in 1890. After cutting and polishing to fully display the contained gold, the specimen won prestigious medals of recognition at the 1893 Columbian Exposition in Chicago and later at the 1900 Paris Exposition. The Colorado Scientific Society donated the "Porter specimen" to the Denver Museum of Natural History in 1977. The museum now displays it with the medals earned in the expositions.

Also on exhibit is the Summitville gold boulder, discovered at Summitville in 1975 by Bob Ellithorpe, and donated the following year to the Denver Museum of Natural History by ASARCO and the Reynolds Mining Company. Some of the specimen's original weight was lost in preparing it for display. The museum had several tiny gold bars, each stamped "Summitville," poured from gold recovered from the "trimmings." In 1990 the Denver Mint reweighed the gold boulder. As now displayed, the specimen weighs 1,592.97 troy ounces, or 81.43 avoirdupois pounds. Gold accounts for about one-fifth of that total weight, 316 troy ounces.

Other notable lode specimens on display at the Museum include leaf and crystallized gold from Leadville's Little Jonny and Ibex mines, Idaho Springs' Dixie Mine, Alma's American Mine, and Farncomb Hill's alluvial Wire Patch, along with gold-in-quartz from

Summitville's Little Annie vein and ram's horn wire gold from the Ground Hog Mine at Red Cliff.

The Denver Museum of Natural History also has the best of Colorado's placer gold—the twelve-troy ounce "Penn Hill" nugget, mined from the high eluvial placers of Pennsylvania Mountain west of Alma in 1937, and the eight-ounce "turtle" nugget, recovered from the same area in August 1990. The Penn Hill and turtle nuggets are the largest specimens of Colorado placer gold known to exist. The museum also displays two dozen fine nuggets for a combined weight of six troy ounces, mined from Cache Creek Park near Granite about the turn of the century. They formed part of the personal collection of merchant and miners' advisor Henry Schutz, and were donated to the museum in 1966 by Schutz's son, Herman.

Jack Murphy, Curator of Geology of the Denver Museum of Natural History since 1970, declines to estimate the monetary value of the collection. Murphy explains:

> Certainly our Colorado gold collection is quite valuable. But that's not the point, because no one can really place a value on heritage. And our gold collection—historically, mineralogically and aesthetically—represents a big part of the heritage of Colorado. A museum's function is not to claim proprietary right; it is to preserve, interpret and publicly display materials that are often irreplaceable.
>
> Remember, too, that while our Colorado gold is sometimes viewed from a historical perspective, the collection itself is not historically static. In just the last twenty years, we've made some major additions. We've brought back "Tom's Baby," and added the John A. Porter specimen, the Summitville gold boulder and the turtle nugget. So we're preserving and displaying more of Colorado's mineral and mining heritage than ever. I believe that when John Campion helped found this museum in 1900, he intended to establish a tradition of growth and continuing service. And that's exactly what we still work toward today.

Museums hold only some of the preserved specimens of Colorado gold. A surprising amount of gold, both lode and placer, is available on the market, mostly through mineral shops and dealers both in and out of Colorado. Many—some say most—of those lode specimens are available because of a Colorado mining tradition that has survived over the decades—high-grading. While some of today's hardrock miners high-grade only to expand their personal collections of ores, most high-graders, just as they were a century ago, are motivated by money. Mines discourage the practice to minimize loss of both work time and gold, but are not always successful.

"High-grading has doubtlessly preserved some gold specimens that would otherwise have been lost in milling," comments Jack Murphy. "But there are two sides to the issue. First, of course, high-grading is illegal. Accordingly, many high-graders obscure or falsify the origin of specimens to protect themselves. Much of the mineralogical value of specimens is in knowing accurately and completely not only district and mine origin, but even the exact level or stope. Therefore, from the museum standpoint, high-graded specimens of any mineral, including gold, are not especially valuable or even desirable, if their origin has been falsified."

The old mountain camps, mining districts, and the mines themselves have also preserved the heritage of Colorado gold. The Colorado Tourism Board has always promoted gold panning and, in its 1991 *Official State Vacation Guide*, asks: "Have you ever really seen purple mountain majesties? Touched a vein of gold?" Each year, many thousands of tourists come to Colorado to do just that—experience the romance and intrigue of the mountain gold camps, tour and photograph the picturesque old ruins, and venture into the mysterious darkness of underground mines to literally touch that vein of gold.

The most historically appropriate route into Colorado's goldfields follows U. S. Route 6 west from the city of Golden into Clear Creek Canyon—the path taken by George A. Jackson and John H. Gregory

*Historical marker in Clear Creek Canyon. Prospectors George Jackson and John Gregory followed Clear Creek into the mountains in 1859 to make their gold strikes.*

on the way to their great discoveries of 1859. On their heels had followed first hundreds, then thousands, of '59ers bound to redeem the Pike's Peak gold rush and to create a territory that eventually became the state of Colorado. Road, rail, highway and tunnel projects have rechanneled Clear Creek, but the legacy of the '59ers and those who followed them remains. Heaps of old placer tailings still line the banks, wooden flumes cling precariously overhead to rocky cliffs and, on most summer days, gold panners by the dozens coax a bit more gold out of the well-worked gravels.

In 1859 John H. Gregory trekked slowly up the North Fork of Clear Creek toward his strike in Gregory Gulch. Colorado Route 119 now whisks travelers toward Black Hawk and Central City, passing more placer tailings, diversion channels, rusting trommels, several fee gold-panning sites, and a number of crumbling, forgotten portals of mines that were driven with hand steels and hammers over 130 years ago. At Black Hawk, an old stamp mill marks the entrance to the Little Colonel Gold Mine, one of the smaller "walk-in" public underground mine tours. Nearby, a simple, often unnoticed, bronze plaque adorns a roadside boulder. Placed in 1932 by the State Historical Society of Colorado, it marks one of the most important sites in the history of Colorado gold:

ON THIS GROUND, LATER KNOWN AS
GREGORY DIGGINGS
JOHN H. GREGORY OF GEORGIA
DISCOVERED THE FIRST LODE GOLD
IN COLORADO ON MAY 6, 1859.
THIS DISCOVERY INAUGURATED THE
PERMANENT DEVELOPMENT OF COLORADO.
THE DISTRICT HAS PRODUCED
$85,000,000 IN GOLD.

Directly across Gregory Gulch is a deep, hollowed, vertical crevice in the sheer rock walls—a crevice once filled with some of the first gold-laden quartz ever mined in Colorado.

A mile further up the gulch is Central City, a tight cluster of Victorian architecture nestled below the mine-scarred hills. The Lost Gold Mine offers a "walk-in" underground tour and the Gilpin County Historical Museum has many mining-related exhibits. Shops and saloons with names like The Glory Hole, The Gold Coin and the Mother Lode line the narrow streets, and an auto tour route winds through the ruins of the old mining district.

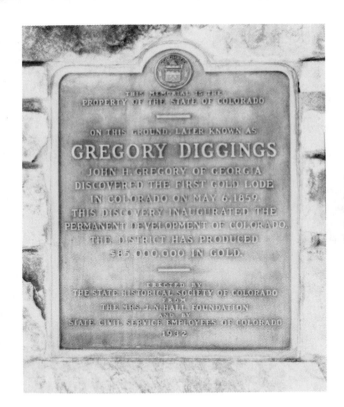

*The plaque marking the site of the lode gold discovery of John H. Gregory on May 6, 1859, on Gregory Gulch.*

In 1859 George Jackson worked his way up the South Fork of Clear Creek toward what is now Idaho Springs. Near the mouth of Chicago Creek, on the grounds of the Clear Creek Secondary School and only a half mile from Interstate 70, is another simple bronze plaque, this one placed into a boulder in 1909, on the 50th anniversary of Jackson's visit.

The leading gold-related attraction in Idaho Springs is the Argo Gold Mill which, between 1913 and 1943, processed $100 million of metals, mostly gold. The underground Double Eagle Mine offers walk-in tours as does the sprawling Argo mill, where visitors can trace the milling of gold ore from the ore bins through stamp mills, mill feed decks, grinding equipment, classifiers, amalgamation tables, flotation cells, concentrating tables and cyanidation systems. Just west of Idaho Springs, the Phoenix Mine offers an interesting tour of a small, working gold mine. Since 1871, the Phoenix has produced several million dollars in gold and silver. Closed by World War II, it reopened in the era of free market gold. Displays include both frontier and modern mining equipment, and visitors can touch a vein of high-grade gold ore, then chisel off a souvenir.

*The plaque marking the site of the first big discovery of placer gold in Colorado by George A. Jackson on January 7, 1859 , near Idaho Springs.*

In Summit County, Colorado's biggest placer gold county, miles of the Blue River south of Breckenridge are covered with evenly stacked, barren dredge tailings, heaps left behind by Ben Stanley Revett and other gold-boat operators. In Breckenridge, the Washington Gold Mining Museum displays relics and historical photographs of the glory days of local gold mining, and those curious to see fabled Farncomb Hill have only to follow a dirt road up French Gulch.

From Breckenridge, Colorado Route 9 crosses the Continental Divide at Hoosier Pass, then descends into the upper drainage of the South Platte River and the Park County mining towns of Alma and Fairplay. Dredge tailings cover large sections of the South Platte channel, and *arrastres* from the 1860s still lie along Buckskin and Mosquito creeks. Fairplay is the site of South Park City, an interesting re-creation of a nineteenth century mining town, and the Prunes Monument, honoring a burro that packed supplies up to the high mountain mining camps and packed high-grade gold ore down.

Leadville, at an elevation of 10,150 feet, is the highest city in North America. The Heritage Museum, near the National Mining Hall of Fame & Museum, has a stamp mill and an extensive collection of

*The "Prunes Monument" at Fairplay is a tribute to all the burros that helped Colorado's early gold miners.*

*The ruins of an old floating bucketline dredge may still be seen in French Gulch, near Breckenridge, today.*

*An* arrastre *dating back to the Pike's Peak rush can still be seen along Buckskin Creek near Alma in Park County.*

memorabilia from the frontier mining era. A marked auto tour route winds through the twenty-square-mile historic mining district, past the ruins of such noted gold producers as the Little Jonny, the Fanny Rawlings and the Ibex, and into California Gulch, site of the richest placer strike of the Pike's Peak rush. Since 1984 Leadville and Colorado Mountain College have staged "Oro City: Rebirth of a Miners' Camp," an annual summer festival of arts, crafts, mining exhibitions and camp-style entertainment celebrating the glory days of old Oro City.

At Cripple Creek, Colorado's most productive gold district, the Cripple Creek District Museum (recognized as one of the nation's finest small museums) has an extensive collection of mining and assaying equipment, claim maps, multi-level glass models of major local mines, and specimens of calaverite, sylvanite and free gold ores. A marked auto tour route leads to Victor and other district towns, past mines including the Cresson, Portland and Ajax, and overlooks the Carlton Mill, where modern gold-extraction technology was born. The Mollie Kathleen Gold Mine is Colorado's only tour mine where visitors can descend a shaft 1,000 feet below the surface. Experienced miner-guides explain underground equipment and workings, including some remarkable mined-out stopes, then provide samples of gold ore.

179

One of the most technically interesting mining-related Colorado museums is the Western Museum of Mining and Industry, just north of Colorado Springs. Visitors are taught gold panning techniques and can enjoy an outstanding collection of both frontier-era and modern mining and milling equipment, some of it in operation.

In Costilla County, near the old Grayback mining district which U. S. Army soldiers mined at least six years before the Pike's Peak rush, visitors can tour a modern, open-pit, vat-leach gold operation. The Battle Mountain Gold Company's San Luis Project, which now produces 50,000 ounces of gold per year, offers tours through arrangement with the company offices in San Luis.

In southwestern Colorado, Silverton's San Juan County Museum displays historic photographs, mining relics and local ores, and

*Fred Garner, veteran Leadville placer miner, at the 1988 "Oro City" summer festival in Leadville. Garner, who made the region's last big placer strike in 1953, still teaches tourists how to find color in the pan.*

commercial jeep tours take visitors into the old mining districts high above timberline. Silverton also offers Colorado's newest underground gold mine tour at the Old Hundred Mine, which dates to 1904. An electric narrow gauge mine train rumbles a third of a mile to an underground hoist room where experienced miner-guides explain mining equipment and methods.

The Ouray County Historical Museum in Ouray has another interesting display of mining relics and photographs. Nearby, the Bachelor-Syracuse Mine, a gold-silver producer dating to 1884, provides another popular underground tour. Mine trains haul visitors 3,000 feet into Gold Hill to see underground workings, mining equipment and veins of gold and silver.

Telluride offers excellent mining displays at the San Miguel County Historical Museum, backcountry jeep tours to timberline mines, and gold-panning expeditions to historic placers guided by a geologist who explains not only proper panning technique, but exactly how the placers were formed. At Ophir, just south of Telluride, visitors can walk 1,000 feet through a tunnel to reach the underground workings of the 114-year-old Silver Bell Mine, then tour the mill to view everything from frontier-era stamp mills and assay offices to modern metal-extraction systems.

At the southwestern end of the Colorado Mineral Belt, 250 miles from the old Cherry Creek gravels, is the San Miguel River, the last major placer stream to be discovered in Colorado. First mined in 1873, the San Miguel River contains gold for its first 70 miles. In Montrose County, just west of Naturita and not far from the Utah line, visitors can still see one of Colorado's most ambitious placer-mining water-diversion projects—the Hanging Flume, built in early 1890s. A "triumph of engineering" that helped produce little gold, the Hanging Flume is still suspended high above the canyon, an unintended monument to the determination of Colorado's placer miners.

*There's still a lot of gold out there to be found. And one thing is no different than it was a hundred years ago. You won't find gold just talkin' about it, you have to go out there and look for it.*

—Fred Garner, Leadville placer miner, March 1991

# 11

# COLORADO GOLD:
# THE LEGACY AND THE FUTURE

Over 42 million ounces of Colorado gold have been mined since William Green Russell washed those first few ounces of placer gold from the gravels of Dry Creek in June 1858. Of the countless thousands of individuals who searched for and mined that gold, a few, including Thomas Walsh, Winfield Stratton and John Campion, made fortunes. Many more found only disappointment and fruitless labor. For most, however, the experience of searching for and mining Colorado gold fell somewhere in between: Their fortunes were never quite within reach; nevertheless, gold, either as color in the pan or a mine paycheck, proved as good a way as any to earn a living.

Gold mining profoundly affected the development of Colorado, its economy, culture and image, leaving a legacy measured in much more than troy ounces and dollars. Gold helped shape modern Colorado, providing landmark technical achievements, displays of glittering specimens, memorable feats of exploration and prospecting, inspiring tales of rags-to-riches, wonderful legends, and quaint mining towns and haunting ruins that seem to whisper of still more gold awaiting discovery.

Colorado is no longer the major gold producer it was at the turn of the century, when it accounted for 38 percent of the huge annual United States output. Today Colorado provides only about 1 percent of the national annual gold production. Yet gold will remain a major part of the historical and contemporary image of Colorado. Few tourists who visit the old mountain mining towns are intrigued by lead, zinc, molybdenum, or even silver. But many are interested in gold and determined to pan a bit of color or touch that vein of gold.

The legacy of Colorado gold, of course, has other sides. Gold mining has contributed heavily to the boom-bust cycle that often characterizes mineral resource development. The brief boom following the Pike's Peak rush led to bust in the late 1860s, then to a sustained boom beginning in the 1880s. Then came bust in the 1920s, boom in the 1930s, another long bust beginning in the 1940s and, finally, the modest current boom sustained by the stable high price of free-market gold. The boom-bust cycle, although usually considered a historical phenomenon, continues to be a part of modern mining. In the late 1980s the modern open-pit mine at Summitville yielded over a quarter-million ounces of gold and provided four hundred employees with an $8 million annual payroll. Although Summitville proved the worth of mass surface mining and advanced extraction methods to profitably exploit very low-grade ores, it provides another example of boom-bust. From start to finish, the entire mining operation lasted only six years.

*Part of the legacy of Colorado gold are hundreds of picturesque old mining ruins.*

*Today, the bed of French Gulch near Breckenridge is covered with dredge tailings, an environmental legacy of the gold boat era.*

Gold mining has also left an indelible mark on Colorado's environment, the consequences of which are only now being fully realized. Until midway through the twentieth century, the prevailing land use mentality in the West, adopted by farmers, ranchers, hunters and loggers, as well as miners, was "use it and leave it." Free use—and abuse—of Colorado's land began during the Pike's Peak rush and later received *de facto* federal approval through the General Mining Law of 1872. The scars left by early mining, including miles of roads slashed across fragile alpine tundra and whole forests reduced to rotted stumps, will never be entirely erased.

Placer mining left hundreds of miles of Colorado creeks and rivers marred by diversion ditches and eroded banks, or covered with lifeless heaps of dredge and dragline tailings. Once a symbol of prosperity, the old diggings are now eyesores that restrict further land use and accelerate erosion. Little of the land disturbed by placer mining has yet been reclaimed. One exception, however, is the reclamation of the Blue River near Breckenridge, where the community uses a large expanse of once-barren dredge tailings for bicycle paths, parks, and commercial and residential development.

Mine-drainage pollution originating in many of Colorado's inactive lode-mining districts is a far more serious environmental threat. Mine-drainage water, characterized by excessive acidity and loaded with heavy metals, is created by the oxidation of sulfide minerals. The most problematic mineral is pyrite, the disulfide of iron commonly known as fool's gold. Pyrite is often associated with precious- and base-metal deposits and is notoriously abundant throughout the Colorado Mineral Belt. When exposed to water and atmosphere, pyrite reacts with oxygen to form sulfuric acid and free iron ions. When the acidic, iron-rich mine-drainage water flows into normal streams, dilution decreases the acidity. The iron then precipitates out of solution as brightly colored iron hydroxide, or "yellow boy," clogging streambeds and staining rocks and banks a telltale rusty orange. Acidic mine drainage often carries loads of other heavy metals, such as lead, zinc, cadmium, copper and silver that, in sufficient concentrations, are detrimental or even toxic to aquatic life.

The water that originally drained Colorado's shallow sulfide ore bodies had naturally elevated levels of acidity and heavy metals. Whatever those original levels were, they were dramatically increased by mining, which exposed billions of tons of mineralized rock to water and the atmosphere in a short time. Miners disposed of the acidic, heavy-metal-laden water by the simplest, most convenient and least expensive method: They allowed it to flow untreated into streams, where the drainage was eventually diluted. Today, thousands of miles of abandoned, collapsed underground workings and

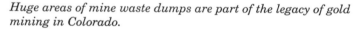

*Huge areas of mine waste dumps are part of the legacy of gold mining in Colorado.*

*Today, mine dumps and ruins cover the area near Leadville's Little Jonny mine, one of Colorado's famed gold producers.*

huge areas of mine waste and mill-tailing dumps continue to slowly oxidize. Together, they create a continuous stream of mine drainage pollution that damages over 450 miles of Colorado streams and rivers.

The convenient disposal of mine drainage water went unquestioned in Colorado for over a century. The government first formally recognized mine drainage as "pollution" in the early 1970s, when the public's growing environmental awareness was reflected in the federal government's establishment of the Environmental Protection Agency and passage of the Clean Water and Clean Air Acts. These actions defined the first national standards for environmental quality. Simultaneously, sharply increased recreational use of Colorado's mountain lands brought new concepts of land use and higher standards of water quality into head-to-head conflict with those of frontier-era mining.

Colorado's most serious and best publicized mine-drainage problem occurred at Leadville, where the effluent from two old drainage tunnels took their toll on aquatic life, including trout population longevity and growth, for over forty miles downstream. In 1980 the Environmental Protection Agency ordered the cleanup of both tunnel effluents. Cleanup of the federally owned Leadville Drainage Tunnel proceeded under the guidelines of the Clean Water Act. The government approached the cleanup of the nearby Yak Tunnel, flowing into historic California Gulch—the site of the richest placer strike of the Pike's Peak rush—quite differently. In 1983 the Environmental Protection Agency designated the privately owned California Gulch area a Superfund site under authority of the Comprehensive Environmental Response, Compensation and Liability Act, legislation aimed at identifying and forcing private "responsible parties" to share in cleanup costs. After a decade of investigation, evaluation of remedial action alternatives, and construction, two water treatment plants began operation in 1992.

The plants are designed to remove over 90 percent of the acidity and heavy metals from the Leadville-area mine drainage, allowing healthy trout to return to the upper Arkansas River. But total cleanup costs have already exceeded $40 million, and annual plant operation will cost an additional $1.5 million in perpetuity. The California Gulch Superfund site has created controversy, since most of its costs were assigned to modern mining companies that the Environmental Protection Agency designated as "responsible parties." Based on costs in the Leadville area, the expense of cleaning up all of Colorado's mine-drainage pollution problems will run into the hundreds of millions of dollars.

Modern mining must now conform to strict environmental codes in exploration, development, production and reclamation. But mining is an inherently heavy-handed process in which significant alteration of the environment is unavoidable. And even in an age of "controlled alteration," the best designs and intentions can go awry, as demonstrated by events at Summitville.

As the Summitville mine was terminating operation in 1991, leaks appeared in the huge, ore-filled cyanide leach pad that was purportedly "impermeable." On September 19, 1991, Summitville made the front page of *The Denver Post:*

MINE'S TOXIC LEAKS RENDER RIVER LIFELESS

DESPITE FINES, PROMISES, CYANIDE FLOWING
INTO ALAMOSA RIVER AND DOWNSTREAM

Deadly cyanide-laced water from a huge gold mine near Wolf Creek Pass has killed all aquatic life in 17 miles of the Alamosa River and the Terrace Reservoir, and it may have seeped downsteam to the Rio Grande, say state and federal officials.

The leaks from the Summitville Consolidated Mining Company continue, despite a $100,000 fine levied against the company this year, agreements to take remedial actions, closure of the once-popular fishing reservoir and complaints from downstream users. . . .

A Colorado Department of Health video of the seepage showed brilliant blue sludge and water—ranging in color from orange to yellow to white to molasses—leaking into the natural waterways from the mine site last summer. . . .

"We've got problems, there is no question about that," [Summitville mine general manager Bill] Williams readily admits, explaining that about 100 gallons of water a minute are leading from the leach pad.

Early mining has also left behind serious hazards. Scattered throughout Colorado's old mining districts are an estimated tenthousand abandoned underground mines. Some are little more than partially filled holes in the ground, while others have headframes, surface buildings and miles of underground workings. Unfortunately, many can still be entered through crumbling open shafts and sagging portals. Abandoned mines—especially gold mines—have long been a magnet for amateur prospectors, self-styled underground explorers, weekend adventurers and curious tourists.

With increasing outdoor recreational activity, more individuals than ever are coming into contact with old mines. Most mistakenly equate them with far more stable natural caverns. In truth, abandoned mines are extremely dangerous. The hazards are not limited to "cave-ins," but include deteriorated ground-support systems, oxygen deficiency, accumulations of poisonous or explosive gases, fire, partially flooded tunnels that conceal vertical workings, and highly shock-sensitive decomposed explosives. Dozens of individuals have been killed, seriously injured or trapped in Colorado's abandoned mines. State and federal funding has already been committed to sealing the old shafts and portals. The project will last decades and cost millions of dollars.

While we can trace the legacy of Colorado gold, the future of gold mining in Colorado is uncertain. Much depends on the state of the mining industry itself. Until recently, American mining remained much as it was at the turn of the century—an oversized, manpower-intensive industry, drawing strength from traditional operating freedoms, a strong domestic mineral market, little foreign competition, and the General Mining Law of May 10, 1872, which permitted royalty-free development of mineral deposits on vast tracts of public land. Its weaknesses rested in increasing obsolescence and operational inefficiency, growing demands from powerful labor unions, declining ore grades, and its obliviousness to emerging environmental liabilities.

189

In 1970, confronted suddenly with mandatory, costly compliance with a host of strict new environmental, health and safety regulations, American mining entered a period of sweeping transition. The long-standing tradition of male dominance in Colorado mining changed in 1972, when women miners began drilling and blasting in the underground alongside their male counterparts.

By 1980 a national economic recession reduced metal demand and prices for silver, lead, zinc, copper, molybdenum and uranium plummeted. Most devastating was American mining's sudden inability to compete in a new international mineral market against foreign mines that enjoyed cheap labor, higher ore grades, fewer operating constraints and, often, government subsidies.

American metal mining all but collapsed, laying off thousands of mine, mill and smelter workers. But the industry survived, buying time and finding desperately needed profits with a single metal—gold. Mining emerged from its depression in the mid-1980s as a restructured industry. It was smaller, less manpower intensive, much more efficient, and adjusting steadily to the new system of operational constraints. Reduced mine employment eroded labor unions' power, and the industry became more competitive in the global mineral market.

The modern American metal-mining industry, however, now faces what may be its greatest challenge: proposed major revisions in the General Mining Law of 1872. Just as intended, the 1872 Mining Law contributed enormously to acelerated settlement and development of the West. Through its location and patenting provisions, thousands of square miles of federally owned land in Colorado and other Western states were transferred to private control and ownership. But the Mining Law has also been widely abused. Federal land has been claimed without the required mineral discovery ever taking place, then used for everything from recreation to speculation, and sometimes sold to non-mining developers for substantial profits.

Although the 1872 Mining Law has been criticized and modified many times, its basic provisions remain. The law has now come under its most serious, concerted attack, not only because of its frequent abuse, but also due to its failure to extract royalties for mineral development on public land. Mining has vehemently opposed the proposed changes, claiming that the Mining Law, as it stands, is the industry's modest version of agriculture's massive federal subsidies and is vital to maintaining the mining industry's competitiveness in a global mineral market. Radical revision of the Mining Law would almost certainly be detrimental to the future of gold mining in Colorado and the West. Because of reduced profit potential, mining companies would hesitate to commit to new projects on public land. A radically altered version of the General Mining Law of 1872 could also mean the end of independent prospectors and small-scale commercial miners, and even of amateur weekend prospectors who continue to stake claims on public lands for recreation rather than development and profit.

The future of gold mining in Colorado faces mixed prospects. Placer production remains at a historic low, with little apparent hope for a significant recovery. In *Gold Placers of Colorado*, Dr. Ben H. Parker, Jr., cities the reasons for the decline of placer-mining. Most obvious is the lack of gravels of sufficient grade to offset the high operational costs of modern mining. Those costs are no longer restricted to digging and washing gravel, but now include posting bonds to assure compliance with strict water quality and reclamation regulations. Water, indispensable for placer-mining, has itself become an increasingly valuable commodity. Conflicting demands by mining, industry, agricultural, municipal and recreational water users has brought lengthy, expensive litigation over water rights that originated with claims staked during the Pike's Peak rush. Placer-property owners often find mining less attractive financially than simply selling out to developers and investors. Finally, proposed placer-mining projects almost always encounter stiff public opposition for aesthetic and environmental reasons. With the odds stacked against it, commercial placer-mining in Colorado will, at best, manage a precarious, token survival.

The future of lode-gold mining in Colorado is considerably better, although it will always depend upon a complex, variable and unpredictable balance of available ore grades, economics, technology and operating constraints. During the 1980s, the stable, relatively high price of gold generated an unprecedented national gold-mining boom. United States gold production soared from only one million ounces in 1980 to an all-time record ten million ounces in 1990. The leading producer is Nevada, which mining professionals have described as "the last, best place for a gold rush." Indeed, most of Nevada's dozens of big open-pit gold mines are located on the remote, arid, sparsely vegetated, little populated and rarely visited Great Basin lands administered by the Bureau of Land Management. Far from highways, national parks and monuments, forests, rivers and resorts, Nevada's gold-mining boom has progressed for a decade with little opposition from environmentalists and outdoor recreation interests.

Like Nevada, Colorado has significant deposits of shallow, low-grade gold ores amenable to open-pit mining and cyanidation extraction. But Colorado also has spectacular snow-covered peaks, deep forests of pine and aspen, thousands of rushing white-water creeks feeding rivers like the Colorado, Rio Grande, Arkansas and the South Platte, and a thriving tourism industry based heavily on natural mountain beauty and outdoor recreation. Not one of Colorado's old mining towns even has a viable mining economy; most have become tourist towns, celebrating and promoting their mining history to attract visitors. The bottom line is that Colorado, unlike Nevada, will never be another "last, best place for a gold rush."

But Colorado does have a considerable amount of gold, as the miners say, "waiting in the ground." Both gold-ore reserves—mineralization that is economic to mine now—and gold resources—lower grade mineralization that may become economic to mine in the future—exist in all of Colorado's lode-gold districts. Most reserves contain only about 0.04 ounces per ton—about the same grade successfully mined at Summitville in the late 1980s—that is now being mined by Battle Mountain Gold Corporation at its San Luis Project in Costilla County.

But the focus of attention for gold mining in the 1990s has now returned to Colorado's greatest gold camp—Cripple Creek. Little modern exploration was performed in Cripple Creek because of the fragmented ownership and control of the district. In 1989, Nerco, Inc., one of the biggest U. S. gold-mining companies, acquired a major interest in the old district in the name of the Pike's Peak Mining Company. Pike's Peak then formed the Cripple Creek & Victor Mining Company, a joint venture with the Golden Cycle Gold Corporation. With control of most of the historic district consolidated, production began by cyanide-leaching of old dump material while exploration geologists embarked on a major drilling program. On September 22, 1991, the *Rocky Mountain News* announced Colorado's latest gold strike:

CRIPPLE CREEK AGLITTER AGAIN WITH
PROMISE OF NEW GOLD RUSH

DISCOVERY, MODERN RECOVERY TECHNIQUES
COULD RE-CREATE BOOM TIMES FOR MINING TOWN

Cripple Creek—Colorado's most storied mining town may soon witness history repeating itself.

This summer's discovery of 1.5 million ounces of gold near Cripple Creek has produced whispers of a gold rush rivaling the town's turn-of-the-century boom. . . .

"I'm sitting on top of the world," said Jim Muntzert, general manager of the Pikes Peak Mining Co. . . .

"There is probably as much gold in the ground as was originally discovered," said Stewart Jackson, a Denver-based independent geologist.

Mining experts sat up in amazement last month when the joint venture reported it has unearthed 518,000 ounces of proven surface gold reserves in the district as well as deposits containing another one million ounces.

The most notable discovery was the Cresson deposit, a 3,000-by-1,000-foot area where 500,000 ounces of 0.04 grade surface gold has been defined. Additional exploration has so far failed to find where the deposit ends.

. . . Since March, the company's payroll has jumped from 55 workers to 128. Mining operations are underway five days a week, 24 hours per day, while heap leaching continues round-the-clock, seven days a week.

To expedite the work, Nerco has shipped in seven 85-ton trucks capable of hauling 40,000 tons of material a day, as well as three 13.5 cubic yard front-loaders.

Plans include spending $3.5 million this year for 275,000 feet of drilling exploration and an additional $2.4 million on a 1,000-1,500-foot heap-leach pad that will hold about 4 million tons of ore. . .

Eventually, Muntzert thinks annual production from the waste dumps and the new finds could reach 100,000 ounces—about as much gold as was produced in all of Colorado in 1990.

"We haven't even started to think about underground production," Muntzert said. "But assume 50 percent of the gold is still there. You're talking about 60 to 100 years of production."

If the geologists are right, Cripple Creek will provide the bulk of Colorado's gold production into the twenty-first century. But reports of a major gold strike no longer guarantee unanimous celebration and untempered excitement. Even with the promised return of big mine paychecks, the changing attitudes regarding mining are apparent.

"In one way it's great to see gold production out of the area," comments Steve Robb, owner of Gold of Cripple Creek, a jewelry shop capitalizing on Cripple Creek's rip-roaring mining history. "But there are consequences. Open-pit mining tends to destroy landscape, and that will take out a big part of history. They'll reclaim it, but it will never be the same."

If the price of gold remains near its 1992 level, Colorado's gold production through the 1990s could rise to 200,000 troy ounces per year, the highest level since the boom year of 1941.

But the days when an individual could strike it rich in a gold rush seem to be history. Future gold mining in Colorado will be a more mundane venture, with lower ore grades, less visibility and less excitement. Nevertheless, the search for Colorado gold, whether by exploration geologists using advanced survey methods, weekend prospectors looking for color in the pan, or tourists seeking to touch those glittering underground veins, will continue.

"There's still a lot of gold out there waiting to be found," says veteran Leadville placer miner Fred Garner. "And one thing is no different than it was a hundred years ago. You won't find gold just talkin' about it. You have to go out there and look for it."

When it comes to gold, Colorado has been and will always be just that—a place "to go out there and look for it."

# SOURCES, ACKNOWLEDGEMENTS AND THANKS

The individuals and sources that played a part in researching and writing the story of Colorado gold are too numerous to mention in entirety. The following includes those which were of the greatest help.

The annual reports, bulletins and papers of the United States Geological Survey, United States Bureau of Mines, Colorado Division of Mines and the Colorado Scientific Society were invaluable. Of special importance were USGS Professional Paper 138, *Mining in Colorado: A History of Discovery, Development and Production* (1926), by Charles W. Henderson; USGS Professional Paper 75, *Geology of the Breckenridge District* (1911), by Frederick L. Ransome; and USGS Professional Paper 610, *Principal Gold-Producing Districts of the United States* (1968), by A. H. Koschmann and M. H. Bergendahl.

Various aspects of the story of Colorado gold came from the following newspapers and periodicals: *The New York Times; Denver Republican,; Rocky Mountain News* (Denver); the January annual mining industry summaries of the *Leadville Herald-Democrat*; Breckenridge *Daily Journal; Colorado Magazine* (Colorado Historical Society); *Rocks and Minerals; Rock & Gem; The Mineralogical Record; The Mining World; Engineering & Mining Journal; The San Luis Valley Historian; The Great Divide;* and the *California Mining Journal*.

Among the most useful books were two excellent overviews of Colorado mining: *Colorado Mining: A Photographic History,* by Duane Smith (Albuquerque: University of New Mexico Press, 1977): and the authoritative work on the state's placer mining industry, *Gold Placers of Colorado,* by Dr. Ben H. Parker, Jr. (Golden: *Quarterly of the Colorado School of Mines*, two volumes, 1974). Other books useful for their coverage of specific localities, historical and economic periods, mining and milling methods, mineral deposits and geology, and related general history include: *The Mines of Colorado*, by Ovando Hollister (Springfield: Samuel Bowles & Co., 1867); *Colorado*, by Frank Fossett ( New York: C. G. Crawford, 1879); *History of Colorado*, by Frank Hall (Chicago: Blakely Printing Co. four volumes, 1880); *Pay Dirt*, by Glenn Chesney Quiett (Lincoln: Johnsen Publishing Co., 1970); *The Past and Present of the Pike's Peak Gold Rush*, by Henry Villard (Princeton: Princeton University Press, 1932); *The New Eldorado*, by Phyllis Flanders Dorset ( New York: MacMillan, 1970); *Leadville: The Magic City*, by Edward Blair (Boulder: Pruett Publishing Co., 1980); *Money Mountain*, by Marshall Sprague (Boston Little, Brown & Co., 1953); *"Uncle Dick" Wootton*, by Howard L. Conard (Chicago: W. E. Dibble & Co., 1893); *Father Struck It Rich*, by Evalyn Walsh McLean (Boston: Little, Brown & Co., 1936); *Colorado and Its Mining Industry*, by O. Glenn Saxon (Denver: Petroleum and Mining Committee, Colorado State Chamber of Commerce, 1959); *Roadside Geology of Colorado*, Halka Chronic (Missoula: Mountain Press Publishing Company, 1980); *Gold: History and Genesis of Deposits*, by Robert W. Boyle (New York: Van Nostrand Reinhold, 1987); *Economic Mineral Deposits*, by Mead L. Jensen and Alan M. Bateman (New York: John Wiley & Sons, volume II, third edition, 1979): *The Extractive Metallurgy of Gold*, by John C. Yannopoulos (New York: Van Nostrand Reinhold, 1991); *Cyanidation and Concentration of Gold Ores*, by John V. N. Dorr (New York: McGraw Hill, 1939); *Clark, Gruber & Co.: A Pioneer Denver Mint*, by Nolie Mumey (Denver: Artcraft Press, 1950); *Across the San Juan Mountains*, by T. A. Rickard (New York: Engineering and Mining Journal, 1903; reprinted 1980, Bear Creek Publishers, Ouray); *Silverton Gold*, by Allan G. Bird (Allan G. Bird, 1986); *Summit: A Gold Rush History of Summit County*, by Mary Ellen Gilliland (Silverthorne: Alpenrose Press, 1980); *Lost Bonanzas*, by Harry Sinclair Drago (New York: Bramhall House, 1966) and *Treasure Tales of the Rockies*, by Perry Eberhart (Chicago: Swallow Press, revised third edition, 1972).

For help in tracing the specimens of Colorado gold that are on display across the country, I'd like to thank Bill Metropolis, Assistant Curator, Harvard Mineralogical Museum, Harvard University, Cambridge; Virginia Mast, Curator, Geology Museum, Colorado School of Mines, Golden; Joseph J. Peters, Senior Scientific Assistant, American Museum of Natural History, New York; Dorothy L. Eatough, Mineralogy Collection Manager, Natural History Museum of Los Angeles County, Los Angeles; Russell C. Feather, Museum Specialist, National Museum of Natural History, Smithsonian Institution,

Washington, D. C., Stephen Bobbitt, Public Relations Officer, and Robert W. Hoge, Curator, World Money Museum, American Numismatic Association, Colorado Springs; and Rebecca Lintz, Assistant Director, Collection Services, Colorado History Museum, Colorado Historical Society, Denver. Special thanks must go to Jack Murphy, Curator of Geology, Denver Museum of Natural History, Denver; and to Carl Miller, President and Executive Director, National Mining Hall of Fame & Museum, Leadville.

Thanks also to Dave Parry, Director, and Mike Bradley, Library Aide, Lake County Public Library (Colorado Mountain History Collection), Leadville; Sharon Moller, Director, Jean Parry, Technical Services Librarian, and Bill Frank, Paralibrarian, Learning Resource Center, Colorado Mountain College, Timberline Campus, Leadville; and to the staffs of the Arthur Lakes Library, Colorado School of Mines, Golden; Research Library, United States Geological Survey, Federal Center, Lakewood; Western History Collection, Denver Public Library, Denver; and the Leslie Savage Library, Western State College, Gunnison.

I'd like to acknowledge the assistance of and thank the following individuals: Allan Bird, consulting geologist and former General Manager of the Sunnyside Mine, Lakewood; Mark Coolbaugh, consulting geologist and former Chief Geologist of the Summitville Consolidated Mining Company, Del Norte; Gary and Barbara Christopher, The Prospector's Cache, Englewood; Fred and Eileen Garner, Leadville; Thomas Hendricks, President, Hendricks Mining Company, Nederland; Dr. Edgar Heylmun, consulting geologist, Tucson; Bruce Johansing, The Mining Gallery, Leadville; Dennis O'Neill, President, Twin Lakes Associates, Leadville; Ron Pochon, independent geologist, Ogallala, Nebraska; Jim and Irene Witmer and the late Gus Seppi, The Rock Hut, Leadville; W. R. C. Shedenhelm, Senior Editor, *Rock & Gem,* Ventura, California; and Kristin Zafuta, Battle Mountain Gold Company, Houston.

Thanks also to Linda Hash and Barbara Morss, Ouray; Digger and Diana Cummings, Mesa, Arizona; Jerry Brown, Cripple Creek; Kathy Blake, Telluride; and Bill and Leslie Jones, Silverton.

I am also grateful for the assistance of freelance editor Mark Waltermire and that of the staff of Mountain Press, especially Daniel Greer, Jeannie Nuckolls, Trudi Peek, John Rimel and Rob Williams.

Finally, I must thank my wife, Lynda La Rocca, for contributing her time and effort to assist in researching and writing the story of *Colorado Gold.*

# INDEX

202

U.S. Geological Survey, 133, 143, 168
United Bank of Denver, 170
United States Mint,
    Charlotte, 39
    Dahlonega, 12, 39
    Denver, 62, 77, 103, 121, 172
    Philadelphia, 25, 29
Unsinkable Molly Brown, 61
Uranium rush, 112
Uravan, 54
Utah, 22
Utes, 5, 49

veins,
    Boss, 57
    Cross, 125-126
    Fountain, 57
    Gold Flake, 57-58
    Hotchkiss, 51, 60
    Key West 57
    Little Annie, 60, 173
    Little Giant, 49
    London, 110
    Ontario, 57
    Smuggler, 60, 69
Victor, 66, 179
Victor Mine, 74
Vietnam War, 117
Volcanic Mining Company, 159

Walsh, Thomas F., 84-86, 138, 183
Wapiti Mine, 92

Wapiti Mining Company, 61
War Production Board, 111
Ware, Col. A. J., 57-58
Washington Gold Mining Museum,
    177
Washington Gulch, 30, 43
Watt, James, 122
Webster Pass, 165
Western Museum of Mining and
    Industry, 180
Western State College, 140
Weston, William, 51
Westport (Kansas City), 9
Wet Mountain Valley, 152
Wightman Fork, 49-50
Wiley, District Judge Jesse, 100
Wilfley Table, 98
Williams, Bill, 6
Willow County, 43, 94
Wire Patch Mine, 57, 59, 172
Wire Patch placer, 57, 59
Wolf Creek Pass, 159
Womack, "Crazy Bob," 66
Wootton, "Uncle Dick," 163
World Columbian Exposition, 60-61
World War I, 98
World War II, 111, 123, 125-126, 133,
    139, 176

Yeoman, J. H., 152

Zebulon, Pike, 6

206